From Cinderella to CEO

How to Master the 10 Lessons
of Fairy Tales to
Transform Your Work Life

CARY J. BROUSSARD

with Anita Bell

WILEY

John Wiley & Sons, Inc.

Published by John Wiley & Sons, Inc., Hoboken, New Jersey.
Published simultaneously in Canada.

For general information about our other products and services, please contact our Customer Care
Department within the United States at (800) 762-2974, outside the United States at (317) 572-3993
or fax (317) 572-4002.

Wiley also publishes its books in a variety of electronic formats. Some content that appears in print
may not be available in electronic books. For more information about Wiley products, visit our web
site at www.wiley.com.

Library of Congress Cataloging-in-Publication Data:

Broussard, Cary Jehl, 1959-
    From Cinderella to CEO : how to master the 10 lessons of fairy tales to
transform your work life / Cary Jehl Broussard with Anita Bell.
        p.   cm.
    ISBN-13 978-0-471-72718-7
    ISBN-10 0-471-72718-0 (cloth)
    1. Women executives.   1. Career development.   3. Leadership in women.   4. Self-actualization
(Psychology)   5. Success in business.   6. Fairy tales—Psychological aspects.   7. Symbolism in
fairy tales.   I. Bell, Anita, 1959-   II. Title.
    HD6054.3.B76 2006
    658.4′092′082—dc22

                                                                                          2005002374

Printed in the United States of America

10 9 8 7 6 5 4 3 2 1

Contents

Contents

Acknowledgments

Where do I begin? I cannot begin to acknowledge all the people who have influenced and impacted this book. But I will start and try to finish before it's time to write the next book.

First, the fairy "godmentors" in my life who made this book possible.

Debra Englander, my editor at John Wiley—you have brought *From Cinderella to CEO* to life. Deb interviewed me years ago about women and travel when she was at *Business Week*. Even years ago, Deb was one of the first to see the importance and impact that women's careers were having on the economy and the changing face and gender of business travelers. When she received our book proposal from Faith Hamlin, my agent at Sanford J. Greenburger Associates, Deb remembered me and the ground-breaking program, WOMEN ON THEIR WAY®. Deb, thankfully there are reporters like you who "get it." You have moved the needle and improved the lives and livelihood of women through your great writing and caring. And most of all, Deb, thank you for taking a chance on me and *From Cinderella to CEO*. Taking risks, as this book supports, is the fastest way to success. I believe this book will be worth it.

To Faith Hamlin, my literary agent, a *huge* thank you. Faith, you are the visionary matchmaker. Faith is the "go to" person for women in the publishing arena. She really has the faith in the ability of women leaders. And she has demonstrated time and again that basic good manners are required in business dealings; if you practice these manners you *will* be a winner—and a leader. Claudia Boutote, who I met through Tamara Gough, introduced me to Faith, and I am extremely grateful. Faith had read my proposal and said, "I like it," then added, "Have I got the magic partner for you and this book!" And her name is Anita Bell.

I like to think of Anita as "Tinker" Bell because she came complete with a magic pen and a whimsical writing style. Anita spins words into gold. Faith, Anita, and Deb: Women like you bring others along, in their careers and in their dreams, and the world will be (and is even becoming) a better place to work—for women and men alike. I know this book is special to all four of us, and indicative of what women do when they work together. And to quote Deb Englander: "We are going to have *fun* with this book."

A *very* special thanks to Fred Kleisner who champions the importance of cultural diversity in the hotel industry. Special thanks to Dave Johnson for believing that a book about fairy tales and career advice would make a great read and to Tamara Gough for urging me to write it. And to all the people at Wyndham for giving me the latitude in my endeavors to create and be successful—especially Judy Hendrick, Andrew Jordan, Elizabeth Schroeder, and Mark Solls for your leadership. And to Mark Chloupek and Robert Solomon, thanks for your encouragement when I needed it most!

There are so many people who have believed in the benefits of Women On Their Way and made it the success it is today. Thanks to the Women On Their Way advisory board over the years, including Adela Cepeda. To all involved with Women On Their Way and Diversity, you know who you are. This book is for you. I have worked with so many smart people over the years and I appreciate all you have taught me. I look forward to learning more with you and those I meet in the future.

This book is also dedicated to my loving husband, Logan René. Thanks for believing with me that *living happily ever after* is a daily possibility. To *all* the Jehls, Broussards, McCaas, and Mathewes family members—thanks for your love and support always. To my sweet friends and associates: Please go to *www. cinderellaceo.com* to see my personal notes to all of you.

And finally to my parents, Louis, Patsy, and Madeleine, too: Thank you for bringing the goodness found in fairy tales into my life and teaching me that there is goodness in everyone—even at work.

In honor of Charles Perrault and the Brothers Grimm, the scribes of so many wonderful fairy tales, and Hans Christian Andersen, who perfected the art of great story-telling. They set the bar for keeping good stories alive.

Introduction

I'M LIVING A FAIRY TALE, BUT NOT THE ONE I EXPECTED. LIKE MANY women, my life didn't turn out to be the storybook I pictured as a girl. But I still believe in fairy tales!

I have always believed that *you can change the world from your desk*. You can make a positive difference in the world as a captain of industry, or even an aspiring apprentice, while still enjoying the rewards of success.

As far as career moves go, I have done well (but confronted lots of wolves and even some evils spell along the way). In the 20 years-plus of my career, I've owned a public relations firm, been a deputy press secretary for the Majority Leader of the U.S. Senate, and even used my public relations tools to help improve the environment—among other things.

However, I did find a way to turn one fairy tale into reality. In 1995, I developed Women On Their Way (WOTW) for Wyndham International hotel company. It was the first branded program to market hotels to women business travelers—and it changed the industry. Starting this venture in the male-dominated hospitality culture was a somewhat controversial move, but it paid off in a big way. I was promoted to senior vice president and helped Wyndham grow from a small chain of 40 hotels to a major hospitality brand. Women travelers now account for hundreds of millions of dollars in revenue each year for Wyndham and other hotel companies, and billions for the overall travel industry.

The cornerstone of the Women On Their Way program, in particular, is the partnerships formed with major women's organizations that support women's business development, careers, and health issues. This has given me the opportunity to travel throughout the country and beyond to speak to women who share my vision of making the world a better place through work.

In 2004, as I was planning this book, I went to Germany on a business trip. Afterwards, my husband and I toured historic sites related to the lives and tales of the Brothers Grimm. It was fascinating to think about how the Brothers Grimm did not *create* their famous fairy tales. They *collected* them—from women! The Grimms traveled the countryside listening to and writing down folk tales that had been kept alive by generations of women who understood their power.

For the past dozen years, I've spent more than half my time on the road, meeting and talking with women from all walks of work life, from CEOs to administrative assistants. And the stories they tell about their careers certainly do rival fairy tales for their drama! Struggle and triumph, despair and hope, loyalty and betrayal, misery and joy—working women face it all and live to tell the tale. What a wealth of experience and wisdom they offer.

The modern heroines of the workplace get picked apart and put down, cast out and lost in the woods, but still they survive and excel. And they don't need a prince to get to the castle. Career women *rescue themselves* through hard work and tenacity. They are not perfect and they make mistakes. They don't always emerge as winners or live happily ever after, but they are still here and making their voices heard—and, I believe, the world is much better off as a result!

Fairy Tales and the World of Work

Fairy tales continue to fascinate because they have layers of meaning that are relevant to anyone, anyplace, anytime. The deeper messages of fairy tales are as significant today as they were 300 years ago. The closer you look, the more you see. And the lessons found within these tales teach us a great deal about work, as well as love.

Fairy tales teach us to be industrious and persistent, and to take pride in doing all our work to the best of our ability. They remind us to treat everyone with respect, to look beyond the surface, and to seek more than material gain. They show us how to deserve and attract the help of mentors (fairy godmothers), cultivate the support of colleagues (including birds and dwarfs), and attain the position we desire—be it queen, manager, or CEO.

Every classic fairy tale has a transformation at its core. From cindermaid to princess, ugly duckling to swan, helplessness to power—these stories tell us that transformation is possible. Translated into today's terms, this means you can wake up from a dead-end job, exercise your inherent power, and transform your work life. You can turn a mundane job into a career that is lucrative, creative, balanced, and satisfying.

Fairy tales teach us how to survive in a volatile economy and fend off the inevitable wolves, poison apples, and evil spells of the business world. And how to find the magic and reward that's hidden in the dark and twisting woods of the workplace. A modern Snow White can thwart an evil queen or backstabbing boss by working hard to win allies. An ambitious Beauty's faith in her choices can turn a Beast into a prince or a manager into a leader. A Gretel thrust into the woods with scarcely a few weeks' severance pay can find her way to a better job. A Rapunzel stuck in a tower or low-paying job can escape and make her voice heard.

And *you* can apply these lessons to transform your own work life!

From Cinderella to CEO gives you the confidence to create a realistic yet passionate vision for your career— and a full menu of tools to get there—because you need more than dreams. You have to support your vision with proven tactics for success. So I've distilled a major lesson from each of my ten favorite fairy tales to guide you on your way.

How to Learn from the Lessons of Fairy Tales

You can choose how to use this book to your best advantage. Read it from cover to cover if you're so inclined. Pick out your all-time favorite fairy tales and see what they have to teach you. Or go right to chapters that offer the lessons and practical techniques you need to solve your particular work issues. Here's a summary of what you'll learn from each story.

Cinderella: Picture Yourself at the Palace and Find a Fairy Godmentor

- Establish a clear picture of how you want to transform your work life.
- Act with the best qualities of a CEO, wherever you stand in the hierarchy.
- Gain the attention and support of an important mentor.

Snow White: Whistle While You Work and Win Loyal Allies

- Master the balancing act of appropriate image in the workplace.
- Work in a way that elicits the loyalty and support of your peers.
- Neutralize envious and unfair bosses.

Little Red Riding Hood: Stay on the Right Path and You Can Fend Off the Wolf Yourself

- Establish your priorities and stay with them.
- Avoid distractions and detractors that lure you off your path.
- Be prepared to fend off enemies with a variety of strategies.

Hansel and Gretel: Find Your Way through the Forest to a New Job

- Recognize signs that your job may be in danger.

- Keep yourself in shape physically and psychologically, especially if you're unemployed.
- Hone your job-hunting skills and expand your network to find your next position.

The Ugly Duckling: Paddle Your Way into a Group That Recognizes Your Strengths

- Identify your strengths and set your sights high even if you face disapproval or rejection.
- Find support within your company and your social/community circles.
- Find and participate in professional support organizations.

Thumbelina: Think Big, Show Initiative, and Do Well by Doing Good

- Do what is right even when you don't have permission.
- Take the initiative and follow your ideas to completion.
- Maintain your integrity and understand the limits of loyalty.

Sleeping Beauty: Be Inclusive and Wake Up to Your Full Potential

- Respect cultural differences and avoid unfair accusations of discrimination.
- Deal with discrimination productively if you're the victim.
- Understand the nuances of sexism and ageism, and get around the barriers.

The Red Shoes: Keep Your Work Life From Spinning out of Control

- Manage your work (over)load with practical techniques.
- Become adept at the techniques of delegation and negotiation.
- Use alternative work arrangements to balance work and family.

Rapunzel: Share Your Ideas and Passion, and Make Your Voice Heard

- Share information, ideas, and resources.
- Get involved in your company's philanthropic side—or create it.
- Find significant ways to make your voice and your ideas heard.

Beauty and the Beast: Stand by Your Decisions, Take Risks and Recognize Opportunity Like a CEO

- Get comfortable making and standing by difficult or unpopular decisions.
- Be the first to spot the potential in products, services, and people.
- Understand your risk tolerance and embrace appropriate risk in your career.

Fairy Tales Are for Grown-Ups

You may be wondering what the topics listed in the previous section have to do with fairy tales. Let me take a minute to dispel a couple of myths.

First, be aware that fairy tale heroines *do not* sit around waiting for their princes to rescue them. Cinderella paid her dues and earned the attention of a fairy godmother/mentor, who gave her a chance to take her place in the palace. Snow White made a niche for herself in the company of seven workaholic dwarfs and inspired such peer loyalty that her dwarf colleagues saved her when all seemed lost. Hansel and Gretel only survived because Gretel had the courage to step up to the plate, take a risk, and shove the wicked witch into the oven.

Another myth that deserves to be cast on the hearth is that fairy tales are only for children. These stories have a long and venerable history. They originated as oral tales that were told to the entire extended family, generation after generation. Versions of stories with similar themes were told in diverse cultures around the globe. Fairy tales are akin to myths—lasting stories with universal appeal and significance. They have always been for people of all ages, including adults.

The first well-known literary fairy tales in the Western world were published in 1697 by Charles Perrault, a French aristocrat, and intended for an audience of sophisticated courtiers. Since then there have been endless fairy tale treatments geared to grown-ups, including feminist, politically correct, and gay-themed versions, literary poems, and novels. In the area of entertainment, there have been fairy tale operas, ballets, stage plays, and art films for mature audiences.

How can the same stories captivate people of all ages and far-flung cultures, from simple rural folk sitting around the hearth in the seventeenth century to the media-saturated public of the third millennium?

The secret is that fairy tales convey basic human truths that never change. They speak to our souls at any age. Their lessons retain their relevance through any cultural shifts, from the olden days when females had very limited options, to today's world of dizzying choices.

Best of all, fairy tales relate their wisdom through stories that are entertaining and *fun*. And that's why I chose fairy tales for imparting important wisdom about work. I believe in mixing business with pleasure. I believe in *getting* pleasure from your business. There's no reason why a book on work needs to be work to read. You can actually learn and retain more when you're having fun.

You can enjoy the modern versions of fairy tales for working women and the fascinating fairy tale lore. You'll hear the stories of many women who've transformed their own careers. You'll learn practical tips for the workplace from experts. I encourage you to soak up the advice you need and put it to work right away. You'll be amazed at how the hidden wisdom of these fantasies will make a big difference in *your* real world.

CHAPTER 1

·····························

Cinderella

Picture Yourself at the Palace and Find a Fairy Godmentor

YES, WE'VE ALL READ *CINDERELLA*—BUT YOU SHOULDN'T DISMISS IT AS a fairy tale of interest only to children. This story has a lot to teach us in today's competitive, cutthroat business world. The new Cinderellas are under constant pressure, but that only builds their strength. They keep working, get right back up, and dust themselves off when they are put down. They make mistakes and are far from perfect. But they are the real heroines of the workplace.

Cinderella is the world's most popular and versatile fairy tale character. Her story has been told in hundreds of different ways all over the globe. Fairy tale folklorists put the number of versions anywhere from 340 to over 1,500! The first and still foremost Western literary version of *Cinderella* was published in 1697 by Charles Perrault, as part of his collection called *Contes de ma Mère L'Oye*, better known as *Tales of Mother Goose*. He introduced the detail of the glass slipper, the pumpkin turning into the coach, and the fairy godmother.

Chances are you know *Cinderella* by heart. But just in case you need a refresher, here is the classic version in a nutshell:

A young girl called Cinderella is cruelly mistreated by her stepmother and stepsisters, ridiculed and forced to act as a

*lowly servant. Yet the girl maintains her sweet and hopeful
spirit, working hard and dreaming of a better life. The prince,
who is searching for a bride, invites all the maidens in the
land to a grand ball. Cinderella's stepmother and stepsisters
conspire to ensure that she cannot attend. However, a fairy
godmother appears just in time to provide Cinderella with a
magic coach, a gown, and a pair of glass slippers.*

*At the ball, the prince falls in love with Cinderella at
first sight. But she is in a hurry to return home before the
magic dissipates at midnight, and rushes off before he learns
her identity. In her flight, she leaves behind a glass slipper.
The prince sends his emissary to find the mystery girl who
fits the shoe. Many maidens try to squeeze into the slipper,
including the stepsisters. But only Cinderella is a perfect fit,
and so she becomes the prince's bride.*

The Brothers Grimm published a grittier version of Cinderella
from an oral folktale called "Aschenputtel" or "Ash Girl." Instead
of a fairy godmother, assistance comes from doves that nest in a
tree Cinderella plants on her mother's grave. The slipper is gold,
not glass, and the stepsisters go to gruesome lengths to fit into
it—they cut off parts of their feet!

In 1950 Walt Disney released an animated film of the fairy tale
that was a huge success, and the movie's graceful, singing heroine
has become our most enduring image of Cinderella. With the
advent of home video, the Disney film is more popular than ever,
and the character has spun off into infinity, with character clothing, costumes, jewelry, housewares—even breakfast with the
"real" Cinderella in Disneyworld's Magic Kingdom. In 2001
Disney hooked up Cinderella with other fairy tale princesses—
Belle, Aurora, and Snow White—forming a quartet that's more
popular than the Beatles, with merchandising sales of over $1.5
billion a year!

But the story of Cinderella is *not*, and has never been, just for
children. Ever since Perrault entertained the sophisticated aristo-

crats of Louis XIV's court with his telling of the story, people of all ages and background have delighted in *Cinderella* variations. The full-length ballet "Cinderella," with music by Prokofiev, premiered at the Bolshoi Ballet in 1945, and charmed an audience of stern Soviet officials. The Rodgers and Hammerstein teleplay, with its unforgettable score, entranced all ages. The literary world has seen an endless stream of adult treatments of *Cinderella,* including a poem by Sylvia Plath, Jungian critiques, and Freudian analyses.

How can one story continue to cut right through the cultural overload and intrigue people of all ages and eras? What is *Cinderella*'s secret?

The Alchemy of Transformation

At the heart of *Cinderella* is the belief in the possibility of transformation. Cinderella is transformed from downtrodden servant to princess, from lonely ash girl to beloved bride. She tells us that everyone, no matter how lowly and scorned, can be elevated. This is the message of *Cinderella* that keeps people captivated. And it applies to working women as well as fairy tale heroines.

Okay, let's get real for a minute. No one is saying that you'll meet Prince Charming and be transformed into a princess and go to live in a castle. (And after reading about the travails of Princess Diana and Fergie, maybe it's just as well.) But you *can* create a realistic and highly satisfying transformation in your work life.

There are as many different ways to transform your work life as there are versions of *Cinderella*—or more. "Women demand a greater sense of fulfillment from our jobs than men do," says Gail Evans, retired executive vice president of CNN and author of *Play Like a Man, Win Like a Woman.* "The standard male-oriented rewards—money, power, prestige—don't necessarily have the same sway with us."

Most of us would like to make more money. But it's not (necessarily) the sole motivation. Some women seek power and an impressive job title, while others aren't comfortable with the high level of pressure and stress that accompany upper-echelon positions. Although this book is called *From Cinderella to CEO,* I am *not* implying that every woman should aim to become a chief executive officer. I am, however, encouraging you to *think* like a CEO in whatever position you hold. And to envision a transformation that suits your own values, goals, and reality.

Some women want excitement in their careers, others stability. Some crave freedom, others prefer structure. Many women seek work that makes a meaningful contribution to the world. Others value a chance to express their creativity. Everyone has a different vision of success. What's yours? You'll need a strong image of how your career transformation will look before you turn the pumpkin into the coach and get there. And no one can create this picture of work fulfillment for you. It depends on your particular balance of values, talents, and desires.

Picture Yourself at the Palace—Step I

Answer these questions to create a clear image of how you want to transform your career.

1. How much money do I need to earn to maintain my desired standard of living?
2. What have I always wanted to do? What's holding me back?
3. Where would I like to work (i.e., at home, in another city, close by)?
4. Am I willing to further my education to be considered for a higher-paid position?
5. Do I like to supervise people? A few or many? Do I feel comfortable in a position of power?

(continued)

Cinderella 5

---

6. Do I like a lot of direction regarding my tasks and projects or do I prefer to work independently?
7. Do I like working in a large, medium, or small company?
8. How important is job security to me? What level of financial risk can I afford?
9. How important is it to me to make the world a better place through my work?
10. How can I help others in a way that is also fulfilling to me, and doesn't sacrifice my dignity or standard of living?

Real-Life Cinderellas

Examples of transformation are all around us. Some real-life Cinderellas are wealthy and world-famous, but others are women you know or even work with every day.

The person who asks to take on a little more responsibility each month, until she gradually works her way into a position of authority and becomes a manager and a mentor for those who come behind her...The innovator who introduces a new concept to the company and keeps pursuing it until the higher-ups listen... The risk-taker who takes the plunge and starts her own business because she has an idea that she believes in...The woman who gets through a difficult situation with a boss, keeps reaching her goals and driving revenue no matter what the company politics may be...They are all Cinderellas.

Christine Duffy started as a project group manager with McGettigan Partners in 1982. Maritz Travel bought McGettigan a few years back and Christine rose to be the CEO of the combined company, which is a global leader in meeting, event, and incentive travel services. "A lot of my rise in the organization was because I was very ambitious," she says. "I was always the one to take on more. I became the one you could give a difficult task to and turn it around. Don't wait for people to suggest you do something," Christine advises. "You have to be responsible for what happens. Get up the nerve to go to your boss and say 'I'd like to take on this project or I think I can make a positive contribution to the company by doing X,Y,Z.' Also, don't wait to be recognized for your abilities. Often being polite and waiting to be recognized is a detriment to women. Ask yourself, 'How do I promote myself?' As Tom Peters says, 'Promote your brand.' Everybody else is!"

Susan Braun is president and CEO of The Susan G. Komen Breast Cancer Foundation, a global leader in the fight against breast cancer through its support of innovative research and community-based outreach programs. "One of the most important parts of being a CEO is seeing the big picture," says Susan. "For women at all levels of business, I encourage them to regularly step back and review how their work contributes to the goals of the organization. Equally important is vision. We all need to envision the end we have in mind, whether it's to create a new business opportunity or cure cancer. If we can see it, we can make it happen."

Picture Yourself at the Palace—Step 2
•••

Use your answers to the questions to write a job description and summary of your ideal work life. Make it as detailed as possible. Include compensation range, hours, type of work, responsibilities, size of company, and so on.

Set yourself up for success, not failure, by developing a vision that it is *possible* to attain. Consider physical limitations, age considerations, and the limits of luck and talent. Also consider your own predilections and personality. For

---

(continued)

example, if you can't stand wearing a suit or working long hours, becoming an executive at a major corporation is unlikely. If you wither in the face of rejection, a career in the creative fields is problematic. But within the confines of your own abilities, there is always room to grow. There is always the possibility of transformation if you design a dream that can fit within the parameters of reality!

Of course, merely wishing that your dreams come true won't cut it in the real world. You're going to have to work hard to make it happen. Be persistent and think like a chess player. Accept your differences and imperfections.

Your imperfection can be the key to the palace. Embrace it, build on it, improve it, find others who appreciate it. Stay true to your dreams and ideals even when you're ridiculed, stifled, or overwhelmed with obstacles. Don't let your mistakes hold you back by dwelling on them.

And make sure to find someone with a magic wand to help you along!

Everyone Needs a Fairy Godmentor

One of the most enchanting qualities of fairy tales is how they illustrate that so many aspects of life remain constant over the centuries. Charles Perrault, who capped his versions of fairy tales with witty *moralités,* offers this insight at the end of his *Cinderella* story: "It is a great advantage to have intelligence, wit, common sense, courage, and good breeding. These and similar talents are gifts from Heaven. But even with these talents, you may fail to reach success, without a fairy godmother or godfather to help you on your way."

Substitute "mentor" for "godmother or godfather" in the last line of this 300-year-old advice and you have an invaluable lesson for getting ahead in today's work world.

I cannot overemphasize the importance of a mentor, or a series of mentors. They have made all the difference in my career. And if you ask almost any successful person, you'll usually find out that she or he was greatly helped by one or more mentors.

Mentoring is as old as civilization. Certainly one cavewoman showed the other how to keep the fire alive and get her fair share of the meat. In the *Odyssey,* Athena, the goddess of wisdom, takes on the form of a man named Mentor in order to give Odysseus advice and guide his son. (I guess the people in those days were so biased they wouldn't take the advice of a female even if she was immortal.)

The modern definition of a mentor is "a wise, loyal advisor," or a counselor, coach, or advocate. The person who receives help was once called a "protégé" but is now deemed a "mentee" in corporate-speak. The word sounds rather like an exotic animal, but in fact being a mentee is a crucial part of growing your career.

"It's not what you know, it's who you know," is a cynical old expression—with a disconcerting element of truth. If you're a woman in business you can change it to: "It's what you know *and* who you know." When you shine doing your work it's always good to have someone to cheer you on. You have to be sharp, well-informed, and at the top of your game. But the reality is that *who* you know also matters, and a mentor gives you a tremendous advantage—if you're willing to listen to your mentor!

Catalyst, the leading research and advisory organization that works to advance women in business, found that four out of five senior women executives emphasized the centrality of a mentor to their success. Sheila Wellington, the former president of Catalyst, points out in her book *Be Your Own Mentor:* "In my experience, the single most important reason why—among the equally talented—men tend to rise higher than women is that most men have mentors and most women do not. Mentors can show you the ropes. And pull strings."

How Mentors Work Magic
....

Mentors can:

1. Teach you specific job skills and procedures
2. See that you get credit for your ideas, efforts, and performance—very important in a mentor!
3. Offer insight into the organizational culture and protection from company politics
4. Provide a safe forum for discussing problems, and a non-threatening form of critique
5. Ensure that you are considered for important projects, committees, and teams
6. Support your bid for a raise, promotion, or desired flexible work arrangement
7. Help you keep things in perspective and maintain a sense of humor
8. Listen (if you listen to them, too)

The Many Faces of Mentors

Okay, you're convinced that you want and need a mentor. But who will it be? You might be surprised.

One of my mentors at Wyndham, Dave Johnson, was younger than I and looked more like a prince than a godmother. *And* we had a somewhat rocky start. Our first encounter was at a company sales retreat during my first six months at the company. The sales and operations divisions were playing a soccer game as a team-building exercise. We marketing executives were the referees. I called the ball "out" during the game when it really *was* out—a good call, I might add! But Dave, a very competitive guy, really "got in my face" for making the call. Sweaty guys started gathering around and peering down at me, all gruff and "p.o.'ed" at me, shoving each other. It was like being in a real live call dispute you'd see on TV, and I was the ref.

Then the CEO came around in a golf cart and said, "Hey Cary, you need to lighten up on your calls." Well, I was mortified and freaked out as well, but I stayed amazingly calm. And I got back in Dave's face by keeping my cool and walking away. Dave noticed my reaction and I won his respect that day. He saw that I wasn't easily intimidated and could hold my own in a tough game. Later that day we laughed about it and he learned I have a sense of humor. And when he became a boss, he decided that I was well worth mentoring.

When you're looking for a mentor, don't limit yourself by expecting your mentor to be a woman. Female mentors can be wonderful, but are often in short supply. Women in senior positions at corporations are a minority and are often overburdened with mentoring requests. Be open-minded and look for a person who's interested and available to you. This person can be within your company or outside it. There are many different types of mentoring relationships, each with its distinct advantages.

The Mentor Boss

These are the most common mentoring relationships since they evolve naturally in the course of business. There are sometimes limitations, particularly in a large corporation, where your immediate report might not have enough leverage to boost your visibility with senior people. You might also find it hard to be entirely honest with your boss about troubling issues. But with the right personality mix and range of opportunities, a mentor/boss can be optimal, providing you a chance to hone your skills on a daily basis and graduate to bigger projects quickly.

If you're in a larger organization, having a senior boss as a mentor sometimes defers advantages over having your immediate report in that role. First, someone higher up may have more clout in supporting your projects and more venues to increase your visibility. Secondly, in case your boss is unfair—doesn't give you credit for your ideas, undermines your efforts, or holds you back—you have somewhere to turn. But beware that you always have to carefully weigh the pros and cons of going outside the chain of authority.

Formal Mentoring Programs

If you have an opportunity to participate in a formal program in your corporation or organization, it's usually worth a try. Not all formal mentors are a good fit and these relationships often don't go as far as ones that develop naturally. They tend to be goal-oriented and limited in scope, lacking the personal connection that makes some mentoring relationships so magical. But formal mentorships can still be a solid way to learn and network. And these programs are being developed and improved by corporations continually.

Multiple Mentors

In 1997, I started a Women's Advisory Board for Wyndham. I had the freedom to hand-pick women from whom I wanted to learn in order to do my job better and benefit Wyndham. Each member of the advisory board is a mentor of sorts, and hearing from these women who are outside the company and free from internal politics has been a tremendous learning opportunity and source of support—and not just for me but for other women and men in the company.

Now, you may not be at a point in your career where you have a chance to create your own board, or even to serve on one. But you can get in touch with multiple mentors by becoming an active member of a professional organization (see suggestions in the "Resources" section).

Peer Mentoring

Leslie Grossman is cofounder of the Women's Leadership Exchange with Andrea March. Their group holds conferences around the country, reaching thousands of women business owners in the million-dollars-plus revenue level. Leslie talks about the value of peer mentoring and how it can evolve: "My first real experience with mentoring was peer-to-peer mentoring as part of an organized, all-female leads group at New York University. Even after that group disbanded we stayed connected. Later one of the women from the original group informally mentored me through the dot-com crash by generously sharing her survival strategies."

Informal peer mentors don't always come through professional organizations. Sometimes they come from unexpected places. Jane Blalock is the owner of a multi-million-dollar company and president of the LPGA's Senior Women's Golf Tour. And she found her mentor through the mailman! "When I started my business it was a woman who helped me, an outplacement person," she says. "The mailman in my office building knew that this other woman was a golfer, and she had an office in the same building, so he said I should meet her. For a year we met once a week for lunch. And she was a perfect business coach to help me."

The Five-Minute Mentor, or Mini-Mentor

Long-term mentoring relationships are the most fruitful, but they can be supplemented with "mini-mentoring." Perhaps you meet someone at a professional conference and have a chance to ask her some questions at the hotel pool. Or you have an opportunity to talk to a senior person in your organization about a specific project or problem. A person can be your mentor for five minutes and it can make a difference. With one sentence of advice I literally changed my life!

Early in my career, when I worked for Peabody Hotels, I was walking down the hallway one day with a general manager for whom I had great respect. He said: "You know, Cary, you can do anything you want in life." No one had ever said that to me (at least when I was ready to hear it) and the comment made a huge impression.

Soon after, I started my own PR firm, and although there was no financial credit available to women at the time who were starting businesses, I just went ahead and did it—without any fear or looking back. The words of the general manager during that spontaneous mini-mentoring session stayed in my mind and gave me a huge boost of confidence.

Family Mentors

Many successful women credit family influences when they are asked about mentors. "My motivation comes from values and ethics that were passed on to me by my parents, grandparents, and others who have chosen to mentor and coach me throughout my life," says Georgette "Gigi" Dixon, senior vice president and manager of national relationships for Wachovia Bank. "Women have served as sources of strength, wisdom, knowledge, perseverance and economic independence through generations in my family."

Your Mentor Possibilities

Write down a list of possible mentors who can help you. Group the candidates into these categories to organize your search:

- Bosses/supervisors
- Peers in your company
- Matches from formal mentoring programs within your company
- Participants in an outside professional development or peer support groups
- Five-minute mentors who might provide "mini-mentoring"
- Family members or friends
- Organizations (see "Resources" section)

Next to each name, write down a first step you'll take to cultivate the mentoring relationship.

You might begin by writing an exploratory e-mail or speaking to someone informally. Maybe you can join a new organization, or volunteer for a committee to get to know a potential mentor. In the case of a mentor/boss, the development of your mentoring relationship is likely to entail more gradual tactics.

How to Attract a Fairy Godmentor

How do you attract a mentor when everyone is so busy and overloaded?

Here's the number one rule of attraction: *Earn* a mentor through your actions.

Remember that Cinderella didn't shirk from her duties, even when they were beneath her station. In the Grimm tale she is obliged to "carry water, light the fire, cook, and wash." In Perrault's story she has to scrub Madam's chamber (including, presumably, the chamberpot) and still be on call to iron her sisters' petticoats. Yet she does it all, and does it well. This establishes her as a person of fine character, deserving of the help of a fairy godmother.

In the workplace, you can't be a drudge or a doormat. You have a right to complain in an appropriate forum if you are required to do tasks outside of your job description on a daily basis, particularly if they interfere with priorities. But you still have to pay your dues, especially if you want to earn the interest of a mentor. Be part of the team and don't always try to be a lone ranger who does no wrong. Real-life Cinderellas are never perfect (and neither are fairy-tale heroines).

Ways to Win a Mentor

Show that you're willing to work hard. The harsh reality of the modern workplace is that it takes a commitment on your part. The people who walk (or run) out the door promptly at 5:00 (at least the first year) are not the ones who attract positive attention from higher-ups. Running into the CEO, CMO, or COO in the elevator after five is a great way to strike up a mini-mentoring conversation and eventually get ahead.

If you are an hourly employee and your company doesn't allow overtime, make the hours that you are at work really count. Remember, perception is reality. When you look like you're concentrating on your job, you're going to get more done. It is a given that the person you want to attract as a mentor is highly focused and hard-working. You must exhibit the same qualities if you want to appear deserving of a mentor's time and attention.

Don't complain unnecessarily. Unless something is highly unfair or inappropriate, don't complain. Remember the expression: "That's why they call it work." It's hard. And it will get harder as you advance, so get in the habit of not complaining. Nobody has the time or patience to mentor a complainer. This is tricky because in the corporate workplace "unfair" may be *de rigeur.* But you need to pick your battles wisely. If you run into a brick wall, develop a new strategy that will turn an unfair situation into a positive one.

Do what needs to be done, not just what you're told to do, and "manage up." Your supervisor is probably too busy to tell you everything that needs to be done. There are times (provided it's not overstepping the limits of your role) that it's good to go ahead and do more than you're asked. But point this out to your boss in an appropriate, effective manner; otherwise, it may be overlooked when it's time for a raise or promotion. Sometimes you can suggest to your boss what needs to be done. If you're juggling two bosses, help them develop a system to clarify your priorities.

Colin Rorrie, Jr., president and CEO of Meeting Professionals International, says, "I am a firm believer in women taking advantage of opportunities within their organizations to volunteer for assignments that may or may not be within their job, that will give them exposure and the opportunity to work with senior-level officers from whom they can gain perspectives that will help them frame their management style."

Demonstrate that you want to learn. Ask for advice—but don't overdo it because people are busy. Participate in training within the company when it's offered. Take outside courses. Read books about your field. Show that you're eager to learn and people will be inspired to teach you.

Alair Townsend, publisher of *Crain's New York Business* and former deputy mayor of the City of New York, says, "One thing I have found to be true: Even the busiest people like to be asked for advice and for help—assuming that the subjects are appropriate. Asking someone tells them their experience and opinions are valuable, that you respect their views, and that they are doing you a favor. And that is very flattering. Plus, most people want to be perceived as sensitive and helpful. So, within the bounds of reason and appropriateness, I believe you should feel comfortable approaching people—and asking for advice."

Nurture Your Mentor Relationships

Short-term mentoring relationships or mini-mentoring can be very beneficial. But longer-term mentors usually have the most impact. Here's how to keep a mentor interested and sustain the relationship.

Accept criticism professionally. Taking criticism is tough. You might want to cry. If possible, wait until you get home. Some believe crying is a show of compassion, but unfortunately, it's more accepted for men to cry in the workplace (although you'll rarely see this happen). When you're reacting to criticism, never get overly defensive. Women are especially prone to losing status when they get defensive. It's not fair, but it's the reality. Sure, you can explain your point of view, but know when not to push it. Timing is everything.

Bounce back and offer solutions. When you have setbacks, keep going. Show resilience. Keep finding alternatives. Be creative about finding solutions. Don't be afraid to show that you have a brain and don't worry that your suggestions might be shot down. I know from my own experience that it's tough to be laughed at or gossiped about. It takes stamina. But if you believe in your work, and you're focused on your goals, you can do it. Be willing to risk failure, and you'll gain the attention and respect of potential mentors.

Strive to make your mentor look good. This is a big one. Longer-term mentoring is a give-and-take relationship. The mentor needs to get something out of it to remain actively engaged. The best way you can do this is by continuing to produce. Ultimately, mentoring relationships must produce a positive outcome and propel *both* people forward.

When you begin to produce significant results, the mentor relationship is likely to evolve. There might come a time when your mentor becomes more of a sounding board or a friend than an advisor. You might be promoted and become a peer of a mentor who was previously in a senior position. Or even get promoted *over* your mentor. And in a small business, you might become your mentor's associate or partner.

Bring Mentoring Full Circle

Once you've established your place in the palace, you can find many ways to do others a good turn. In a corporate setting, you can support your former mentor's projects and initiatives. If your mentor has her own business, share networking contacts and send her new clients. You can also become a mentor to other people and pass on the wisdom. Often the most dedicated mentors are those who had a pivotal mentor earlier in their careers.

Judi Hampton, who had a stellar 17-year career at the Mobil Corporation before starting her own company, explains: "I was doing 'gopher' work when my boss, who was also my mentor, talked management into letting me try out to be a TV spokesperson. He was always there as an advisor, a cheerleader, a supporter.

My visibility went up one hundred percent and I became senior spokesperson to all media and director of consumer affairs at Mobil." Judi went on to manage the Mentor in Engineering program for minorities at the Mobil Corporation. She later started her own training company, where she coaches and mini-mentors hundreds of people a year.

It's very exciting when mentoring comes full circle. I can honestly say that creating a better environment for other women in business is the most rewarding part of my job. And remember, if you're a true heroine, you'll stick to *positive* payback and not waste your time plotting revenge.

Doing Well Is the Best Revenge

The original Perrault and Grimm versions of *Cinderella* don't actually include the words "happily ever after." Very few fairy tales do. Instead, the two classics finish with the stepsisters' fate, although they tell two very different tales. The Perrault story ends by saying that Cinderella, "who was as good as she was beautiful," took her sisters to live in the palace and married them to two great lords of the court. In the Grimm version the doves take matters into their own beaks and peck out the stepsisters' eyes. Nonetheless, Cinderella is not the one who punishes the stepsisters. She's too good to waste her time on revenge. And so are you.

If you want to tell someone off, write the miscreant a letter instead, with an important caveat—don't send it. Put it in the shredder. If you have an enemy in the company, let him or her self-destruct. People who are really nasty usually do. If not, you can choose to *ignore* detractors. Nothing deflates people faster than acting as if you don't care what they think or do. Focus on finding and cultivating supporters instead of dissipating your energy on revenge. Be professional and be forgiving. But don't expect others to forgive. Some will harbor deep resentment—it's a reality. But you can keep your head above the fray and set your sights high.

· ·

Twenty-First Century *Cinderella*

Once upon a time, a bright and ambitious young woman went to work as an administrative assistant for a large corporation. Although it was an entry-level job, the VP who hired her promised that she would have an opportunity to advance in due course. But soon it became clear that the VP left everything to an evil department manager, who favored two other administrative assistants whom she had hired. The bright young woman was given the most tedious tasks to perform and spent so much time in the copy machine room that the toner was always rubbing off on her clothes and getting stuck under her fingernails. And so they called her Cinderella.

One day the CEO of the corporation sent an e-mail to all employees, inviting them to a grand meeting to be held in the ballroom of a lavish hotel. The CEO invited everyone to enter a contest by writing a speech on how the company could experience double-digit growth in the next decade. The winner was to present the speech at the meeting.

The two other admins took long lunches and left work early so that they could shop for designer suits and shoes to wear to the big event. They dumped their work on Cinderella to finish. Yet when Cinderella complained about their wicked ways to the department manager, the boss snapped: "You'd better exhibit more team loyalty next time. Now get back to your cubicle!"

So every evening after Cinderella had finished the selfish admins' work and her own she remained at her desk after hours, fine-tuning her submission for the corporate contest. No matter how undervalued and overworked she was right now, she could still picture herself at the podium. The nighttime security guard would shake his head in sympathy at the sight of Cinderella toiling far into the night.

The day of the grand meeting, Cinderella was planning to look for a new outfit at a sample sale during her lunch hour. But the department manager dropped a bombshell on her desk just before noon. "Take these notes and organize them into a formal report," she ordered. "And have it on my desk by tomorrow morning or you'll pay in your performance review!"

Poor Cinderella had to work through lunchtime, and stay in the office after five, trying to compile the report. But the data was so convoluted that she couldn't make sense of it. Finally, she dropped her head on her desk, weeping in despair.

Just then an elegant woman carrying a garment bag entered the office. "I've been watching the way you keep on plugging when the going gets tough," she told Cinderella, "And I've decided that you deserve my support. I'm going to be your fairy godmentor, so to speak. I was the first woman to be named to the board of this corporation and I still wield a lot of influence."

"I only want to go to the company meeting, and have my submission chosen on its own merit," Cinderella said. "But now I'll never have time..."

"Think like a CEO. Concentrate on finding solutions," said the godmentor. "The security guard moonlights as a livery car driver and he's waiting outside to take you."

"But I have nothing to wear," said Cinderella.

"We'll take care of that. There's always a way if you're a change agent." The mentor took from the shopping bag a couture suit of the finest white wool, with silk lining and gold chains at the waistband. "This will be perfect for you. And I've always felt that accessories are the ideal way to show a little individuality while still maintaining an appropriate professional look." And she showed Cinderella a pair of fabulous plexiglass pumps.

Cinderella slipped them on. "Wow, you don't know how much trouble I usually have finding shoes that fit. I'm a size 10 narrow!" she said.

"No problem. Now get yourself changed and be on your way, my dear. But don't go out for drinks after the event. Be home by midnight so you can be well-rested and ready to work tomorrow by nine sharp."

The ballroom of the grand hotel was filled with a thousand employees, all dressed in their finest clothes and on their best behavior. After the keynote address, the CEO of the corporation announced the winner of the contest. It was Cinderella! As if in a dream she floated up to the podium to give her speech. At the reception afterwards the CEO toasted Cinderella with a flute of champagne and told her: "You have some excellent ideas for the company. And you had real executive presence at the podium. I was impressed the minute I heard you." Cinderella was invited to sit next to the CEO at the reception and was introduced to everyone as an up-and-coming talent.

The evening passed so quickly in a whirl of clever finger foods and networking that Cinderella almost missed her midnight deadline. When she noticed the time, she ran out of the ballroom so swiftly that one of her shoes fell off. Later, she realized she had not given the CEO her name or signed the speech because she was afraid of retaliation by her boss.

The next day an e-mail went out to all the employees of the corporation saying that the CEO was seeking to identify the employee who wrote the winning speech. And to prevent anyone from stealing the credit, the winner must prove her identity by fitting into a certain size 10 narrow shoe.

The two other administrative assistants in Cinderella's department went into a tizzy. One of them booked an emergency appointment with a plastic surgeon who specialized in foot surgery for women who wanted to heighten their arches to fit into stilettos. The other admin flexed and pointed her feet 500 times day to lengthen her instep. Cinderella just concentrated on doing her job.

When the VP made it down to their department the following week to see if anyone could fit into the plexiglass pump, the first admin was still swelling from surgery and didn't have a prayer. The other coworker was seized with a foot cramp, snapped at the VP, and burnt bridges. But Cinderella calmly slipped her extra-long foot into the striking yet sensible shoe. To seal the deal, she produced the second glass shoe from her padded laptop case, where she had put it for safekeeping.

Cinderella was immediately promoted to a growth position, where she was able to make her mark. One of her first projects was to start a mentoring program that was open to all employees, including the chastened admins and the security guard/driver.

And over the years, Cinderella always displayed the plexiglass shoes on a credenza in her office as she worked her way up to CEO.

....

Fairy Dust from *Cinderella*

- Behave as if you belong at the ball. Display the best qualities of a CEO, wherever you are in the hierarchy.
- Believe in the possibility of transforming your work life. Take inspiration from real-life Cinderella success stories.
- Picture yourself at the palace. Understand what success means to you and develop a detailed vision of your ideal work life.
- Earn a "fairy godmentor" through your actions. Cultivate the right attitude and work ethic to attract a series of significant mentors.
- Bring the magic full circle. Make your mentor look good. Then become a mentor yourself to someone deserving.
- Never diminish yourself by seeking revenge. Hold your head high and you'll deserve to wear the crown.

....

CHAPTER 2

Snow White

Whistle While You Work and Win Loyal Allies

SNOW WHITE IS ONE OF THOSE FAIRY TALES THAT MAKE POSTFEMINIST moms worry about imparting the wrong bedtime message, largely because of the misconception that the prince saves Snow White with a kiss. However, the real story is that her new friends, the dwarves, save Snow White, and she inspires their loyalty through diligence and teamwork, not her pretty face.

This fairy tale illustrates the importance of developing allies by making yourself valuable to your coworkers. Snow White shows us that being the object of envy can be dangerous, but with the strong support of coworkers, it is possible to make it through, even when your adversary is in a position of power.

The tale of *Snow White and the Seven Dwarves* was told around the hearths of countless cottages in Europe before it was first published by the Brothers Grimm in 1812. Then the story was selected as Disney's first full-length animated fairy tale film and released in 1937 to universal acclaim. The film relied heavily on the Grimm version and didn't shrink from scary details, such as the demand by the queen that the huntsman deliver Snow White's heart to her—on a platter! But there are a few crucial differences. In the old-style fairy tale the dwarves have no names and are humorless work drones, while in the Disney version, the dwarves steal the show, with their cute names and personality quirks. Also, in the Grimm version Snow White is only seven years old when she is cast out by the queen, and there is no mention of how many years pass before she is taken by the prince. In the Disney film, Snow White appears to be a teenage maiden, making the romantic aspect of the story more palatable to modern audiences.

Here is a quick summary of the classic fairy tale, in case you need a refresher. (I've left out the bells and whistles, so by all means go back to the original versions of this and other tales when you have the time. You'll find them fascinating!)

> *Snow White's stepmother, the queen, is consumed with envy when her magic looking-glass tells her that Snow White is fairer than she. She orders her huntsman to kill Snow White, but he takes pity on the girl and spares her life. Lost in the woods, Snow White comes upon the cottage of the seven dwarves. They agree to allow her to live in their cottage if she cooks, cleans, and keeps house.*
>
> *When the queen finds out that Snow White is still alive (and still the fairest in the land), she attempts to kill her three times. On the third try she tempts Snow White with a poisoned apple, and the girl falls down dead. The devoted dwarves can't bear to bury her, so they keep her in a glass coffin. A prince falls in love with Snow White and orders his servants to carry her coffin to his castle. As the prince's servants are carrying Snow White's coffin away, they stumble and jolt the coffin, whereupon the piece of poison apple flies out of her throat and she comes back to life. Snow White marries the prince and the queen suffers a dire fate.*

Notice that in the original story it is not the prince's kiss that wakes up Snow White. This myth that we were raised on was actually started by Disney. In the old version, it's a quirk of fate that the apple is jarred from Snow White's throat while her coffin is being moved.

The Message in the Mirror

Snow White raises some interesting questions about the advantages and dangers of beauty. First, the queen's jealousy over Snow White's appearance ignites her murderous wrath. Then the huntsman spares Snow White because of her beauty and innocence. But the dwarves provide the most insight into how people usually react to beauty in the *workplace*. When the dwarves first discover Snow White asleep in the cottage, they are so happy to admire her beauty that they don't wake her. But she cannot get by on her looks alone for too long.

After she wakes up and tells the dwarves her sad saga, they respond: "If you will keep our house for us, and cook, and wash, and make the beds, and sew, and knit, and keep everything tidy and clean, you may stay with us." "With all my heart," Snow White replies. And she makes good on her promise, keeping everything in tip-top order for the dwarves so they can concentrate on their long days at the gold mine. Talk about workaholics! It is Snow White's work ethic that wins the dwarves' loyalty and ultimately saves her.

Applying this scenario to the workplace today, there are certainly some professions in which looks are paramount, especially in the fashion and entertainment industries. But in general, women should not coast on their beauty or sexuality—and very few try. It is a TV-sponsored myth that businesswomen are stiletto-heeled vixens in minisuits. In fact, most women know that an overtly sexy image can actually *reduce* status and reputation in the workplace. Nonetheless, it is human nature to gravitate toward good-looking people, and an attractive appearance is a *definite* asset.

How you dress and present yourself is a balancing act. You have to be conscious of the messages that you send by your clothing, makeup, and mannerisms. And, what constitutes proper attire is complicated because there are so many variables. The days of women hitting the workplace in cookie-cutter knee-length skirt suits with bow ties and shoulder pads are long over. The rule book has been tossed in the shredder.

This diversity in business dress follows a wider trend of eclecticism in fashion. There's no longer one acceptable hem length, standard silhouette, or definition of what's "in" and "out." Fashion consumers are seeking ways to customize their dress and look unique.

In one way, this trend is a relief. I remember how utterly bored I was with the endless gray and blue suits, pearls and pumps that were standard issue in my earlier career. Now there is a wider range of acceptable workplace attire and we don't have to look like drones. Yet these choices can be confusing because we still have to be careful that we're projecting an appropriate image.

The goal is to develop a look that gives you confidence and encourages others to take you seriously. We can rail and cry that looks shouldn't matter—but they do. That's the reality.

During my college years I was a blue-jean wearer all the way. One week our women's association from the University of North Carolina (UNC) went to a conference at the University of Miami of Ohio, where one of the speakers made a big deal about how important it was to dress well when we entered the business world. I chose to question her advice, saying that I thought it was the person that mattered, not the clothes. I was naïve.

I still believe that the work itself is paramount. But why handicap yourself? Appearance alone will not bring you success, but the wrong look will definitely hinder your progress. I've experienced it firsthand.

I have always tried to look professional, and I work extremely hard. But about a dozen years ago, I was feeling stalled. I was producing terrific results, but not getting the recognition I deserved when it came to salary and title. When it was time for my performance review, my boss said to me, "You're doing a great job, but you need to improve your appearance." I was shocked! I didn't even have the composure to ask my boss specifically what was wrong with my appearance (although I later wished I had).

Back home, I cried, stormed that it was unfair, and talked to my husband about the problem. Lucky for me, he's not only consoling, but also good at figuring out rational solutions. Well, there was a personal shopper who had been sending me promotional mailings (which now made me paranoid—had someone asked the personal shopper to send me the "teasers?"). Anyway, I swallowed my pride and contacted the personal shopper to help me find clothes and choose an updated "do." I wore those new clothes with confidence and went on to become a vice president. Of course, it wasn't the clothes that got me the promotion, it was hard work. But the right look certainly helped.

Even if you have a limited budget, there's always a lot you can do within your own parameters. Men have been pulling off average-budget work clothes for years now. You don't need designer labels to look polished and successful. If you have the right attitude and pay attention to grooming and details, you can pull off a CEO look on a modest salary.

Pay Attention to Details

When you're planning your professional look, start at the top. For women, hair presents a vast array of choices. There's only one hard and fast rule about hair for the workplace: Keep it in shape. Get your hair trimmed frequently enough so that it maintains its style, whether long or short. Pay extra attention to a good haircut if you're busy and don't want high-maintenance hair. Keep it clean and shiny, of course. And keep an eye on your "roots" if you dye your hair.

I go back and forth between keeping my natural silver/gray color and dying my hair. Surprisingly, the natural color seems to be more controversial. Some people just can't understand why a woman in her forties would let her hair "go." On the other hand, I've had people I respect say to me, "Cary, you look great with silvery hair; it's part of your 'brand magic.'"

You can't please everyone all the time. Look at how much controversy Hillary Clinton stirred up with her changing hairstyles. Just consider the message that your hair color and style convey, and make sure it's right for your position and industry.

In most jobs, it's best to save the dramatic makeup for private life and stay with a moderate look. Be sure to check your makeup under the office lighting to see how it translates. Ask for some help at the makeup counter and explain that you want a look appropriate for the office. When it comes to nails, steer away from decals, superlong talons, and anything else that will distract people from your ideas and professionalism. Be careful with dark nail polish because it is harder to keep maintained. A chip on a crimson nail looks tacky, while a slight flaw on a French manicure or pale pink can go unnoticed.

It's curious that the evil queen tried to trip up Snow White with *accessories*—twice! First the queen tempted Snow White with colorful silk bodice laces and laced the girl so tightly that she couldn't breathe. Next, the queen tricked Snow White into opening the door by luring her with a poison comb.

Accessories are also significant in business attire, and figuring out what works can be a killer since there are so many factors to consider. A big diamond ring can get you a long way in one city but may be considered ostentatious in another town. A group in Washington, D.C. might expect your handbag to match your shoes, while in New York all that's expected is style and flair. Besides the geographic differences, corporations, nonprofits, and academia all have their subsets of taste.

Jewelry sends a message about your taste and affluence—but who's to know if it's real or not? A couple of years ago my house was robbed and the thieves took a pair of fake diamond earrings and rings. Even the "pros" couldn't seem to tell the difference! Stars have been wearing pastes of their jewelry for years in public.

Details count right down to your toes. For decades the standard was a pump in a dark color with sheer pantyhose for business. Now there's more variety—in some industries and some cities. Many offices have casual Fridays or casual seasons when it is acceptable to skip the hose. But as much as I'd love to be free of the darn things, in most situations they are standard business attire.

I always feel more confident if I know I'm suitably attired for any business situation—but I'm not always—and when I get "caught" because a client or colleague drops by, I always wish I had taken a little time to polish my look. I get tired of the effort it takes, of course, but I find that purchasing a few things that are extra comfortable, yet look crisp and professional, is invaluable.

Even when you've gotten a handle on accessories, clothes have been known to trip up many a capable woman. As much as it's fun to charge ahead to the mall and buy something that catches your eye, you're better off with a little planning. Then you won't end up with a closet full of clothes and nothing to wear to work.

Different Looks Fit Different Fields

- Creative fields such as advertising, entertainment, and fashion offer much more leeway in dress.
- If you're in sales, dress in a way that impresses your customer. Think about your customer's taste, not just your own, and how you represent your product or company.
- If you're in a teaching, social services, or government position, it's nice to set a good example. You don't have to be a fashion plate or look corporate, but your clothes should be tasteful, efficient, and pleasant.
- Financial services and legal professionals are generally conservative. Top-quality fabrics and a good fit are crucial.
- Corporations vary widely. Look to women who have been with the company for some time to see what type of dress is favored.
- If you're not sure what's acceptable, it's always a good idea to err on the side of good taste. The goal in business dressing is to feel 100 percent confident.

Know the Lay of the Land

Different parts of the country have different standards. Forgive the stereotypes, but we all know New Yorkers wear a lot of black; Californians tend to show off their fit figures; women in the South wear more bright colors, pastels; and so on. That doesn't mean you can't break the mold. But remember the saying, "When in Rome, do as the Romans do."

Express your originality within the sphere of what people in that region find attractive and appropriate. Take time to stay up on trends, but don't be afraid of adopting a signature accessory, hair color, or other style detail—provided you can pull it off. After all, what would Cinderella be without her glass slipper, or Little Red Riding Hood without her red cape?

Dress "Up" for Success

If you work in a large corporation, take notice of what people at different levels wear. There may be different standards and expectations for support staff or management. Always dress at or above your level. Dressing "up" above your current job level can help people see you as someone who can handle more responsibility.

Irene Malbin, vice president of public affairs for the Cosmetic, Toiletry, and Fragrance Association suggests: "Look professional and competent—like you would want the company to be represented if you owned the company, because one day you may in fact be the CEO, or own the company."

Within the same corporation, there will often be different looks in different departments. Casual and quirky may be fine in the graphics department, but not in accounting. You can stretch the limitations a little and add your own touches, but it doesn't pay to be a major clothes rebel at work. When you don't dress the part, people begin to wonder if you belong in that role.

Fortunately, women don't have to try to look like men in skirts anymore. Woman at the top who exercise their authority on a daily basis are not afraid to look feminine. Michelle Peluso, president and CEO of Travelocity, says, "For years women were afraid of being 'female' in the workplace. I think we are finally coming into our own and can be ourselves. Women in general have a much wider array of styles to work with as they manage, which is a real asset. I can slam my hand on a table and tell someone to take a hike in negotiations, but I can also be very traditionally female in other situations. The most important thing is being authentic to your own style."

Know Yourself and Be Yourself

Are you young or middle-aged? Short or tall? Thin, large, or medium? Know yourself, accept yourself, and be sure that the styles you select are appropriate and flattering. Another question concerns personal sense of style and taste. It's simplistic to insist that you want to "be yourself." You need a style in which you feel comfortable and true to yourself. But the business world is not a vacuum. If you want to impress other people and move ahead, you may have to adapt your style.

Patricia "Patty" Francy, treasurer and controller of Columbia University, says: "When I was starting out in my career, I thought if you delivered substance, form did not matter. One boss harangued me to stop wearing green leather pants and sandals to work and dress for the boardroom. I changed my position to substance *and* form. I am now in the boardroom." In fact, Patty Francy is in many boardrooms: She's a director of the Siebert Financial Corp., the Women's Financial Network, the Women's Economic Round Table, and priceline.com. Although Patty does not back down on tough issues in the boardroom, she had the sense to compromise on attire—at least in the workplace. (By the way, if anyone could pull off green leather pants in the office, Patty could!)

Quality Counts

I recommend investing in one or two very high-quality outfits, the best you can afford. The same applies to your jewelry selections and your shoes. Times change, styles change, but classic looks always work. These investments will take you through important meetings and public appearances with an enhanced sense of confidence.

You will need to do a little homework on the subject of quality, because labels can be deceiving. Some famous designers come out with trendy styles that won't last through two seasons. If you're investing in something expensive, be sure it has staying power. The safest investment is a suit made of wool, wool blend, silk, or silk blend.

Designer or couture suits feature outstanding quality, but are too expensive for most of us. "Bridge" lines (which are found in the designer sections of many department stores) are the next step, less expensive but offering fine quality in cut and fabric. Another category is "better" career clothing, which provides good quality at lower cost.

Shop extensively to find the most flattering style of skirt and jacket for your body type. Don't buy anything too short or tight, even if you just spent six weeks on a diet and lost ten pounds. Save the purchase that is a size smaller than usual for something trendy and inexpensive. Buy a size that you'll be sure to fit into for years to come if you're investing in a top-quality suit.

Outside of your one or two superior suits, you'll need a minimum of six outfits that you can wear to work with confidence. A mix of pants and skirts with jackets and blouses that match is most practical, although you might want to throw in one or two dresses.

Caution: Figure out what piece goes with what before you buy. If you need help, ask someone who has good taste to come along: a girlfriend, boyfriend, husband, partner—sisters and mothers never lie! Some stores also provide personal shoppers free of charge. Just make sure that the emphasis is on finding pieces that work together, rather than being swept away by a jazzy separate that doesn't go with anything.

Create Your Classy "Castle" Wardrobe
....

Answer these questions to analyze your working wardrobe needs.

- How would you describe your business if you had to choose one of these words: conservative, liberal, creative, serious, entrepreneurial?
- In which part of the country is your work? Do you work in a large city, a suburb, or rural area?
- Is your position on the creative side, marketing/sales, research, or financial?
- How do your female coworkers dress for work? Your female bosses?
- Do you work with the public? Do you sell? Do you meet with clients or customers?
- What styles are most flattering for your figure?
- Do you have at least one high-quality business suit?
- Do you have six outfits that you know are appropriate for work?

Write a list of the clothes that you know work for work. Then write down a list of the missing pieces.

How to Survive a Wicked Boss

In the story of *Snow White*, the queen is struck by a frenzy of jealousy when the mirror says: "Queen, you are full fair, 'tis true, but Snow White fairer is than you." In the workplace, talent, ambition, energy, results, and recognition are more likely to cause jealousy than sheer beauty. And the wicked "queen" can be male or female, younger or older.

I believe it is an evil myth that older female bosses are often jealous of up-and-coming women in their companies. It happens, but it's rare. Jealousy and competition between women in the workplace is exaggerated and often used as a tool to point fingers at women who may be locked in a disagreement or have butted heads on an issue. Even though two women take two different stances, it doesn't mean they're ready for a catfight. Men tend to want to "fix" any disagreements between women instead of letting them solve them on their own.

More often, older women, who may have experienced more sexism and roadblocks as pioneers in the business world, are pleased to see younger women getting ahead. This doesn't mean that jealousy and undercutting by senior people isn't a concern. But the evil queen might be a man.

Snow White, despite the warnings of the more seasoned and cynical dwarves, allows the evil queen to trick her again and again. This is understandable considering her youth. But for a woman old enough to be in the workplace, it is out of the question.

You cannot allow yourself to be a victim. You cannot be an unwitting enabler.

Sometimes women have a hard time accepting how ruthless people can be in the world of business. Most men accept as fact that the power play is fair play, but sometimes women choke on the truth. And it's especially difficult when it's a person in a position of power who has it in for you. You must be ready to respond with a number of strategies.

Seven Survival Strategies

Snow White had the Seven Dwarves to help her survive the cutthroat queen. You are going to need a versatile range of techniques: the Seven Survival Strategies for keeping your job and reputation when you have a difficult boss.

Strategy #1. Whistle while you work and win allies. Remember, the dwarves were the ones who saved Snow White when she was down. And it wasn't her pretty face that won their loyalty, it was her hard work. She didn't groan and moan about working as a housekeeper, even though she was born a princess. She did her work cheerfully and made herself indispensable to the dwarves. And that is what you need to do at your job.

Never make the mistake of thinking that only higher-ups can help you. Winning the respect of your peers—and even coworkers who are lower in the company hierarchy—is always worthwhile. If you're having difficulty with your immediate boss, a human resources manager or a senior boss will often consider what others say about you. Peer support can be instrumental in saving your situation. Fortunately, many women have an innate talent for expressing the empathy and interest that builds peer relationships.

"As women, we have in our nature and in our nurture to be great connoisseurs of relationships," says M.J. Calnan, managing director of the Women's Leadership Initiative of Meeting Professionals International (MPI). "From the time we are small, we are involved in taking stock of what's happening around us. At the 'playground' seeing who the important 'girls and boys' are is a wise thing to do, and as adult women, too! Who is this person that can help us in our quest? How can I build a relationship? What do she or he and I have in common? How can I build a bridge over to where she or he is?"

Strategy #2. Strive to win the boss over with sheer excellence. You might be able to inspire an attitude adjustment by delivering outstanding results. Your results can make your boss look good and win him or her over. At the very least, your accomplishments will make it easier for you to defend yourself with higher-ups, and either save your job or move to a different position in the company. Be sure to keep a careful record of your work and efforts. Selectively distribute memos and reports that document your results. Documentation is an important weapon if you need to defend your position.

Sometimes a boss will mellow out after you prove yourself. Justine, a project manager for a large corporation, had a supervisor who was intensely demanding and never satisfied with her performance. Then the boss took six weeks off to deal with a family matter. During this period Justine came through for her boss, troubleshooting several different crises and keeping the projects on schedule. When the difficult boss came back, the relationship was on a different footing. Justine had gained her boss's trust by stepping up to the plate in her absence (without treading on her boss's territory). Her boss did not feel threatened, yet Justine had made her look good and won points and trust. The boss who had been an adversary became her supporter, recommending her for a salary increase and promotion.

Very often a boss will be tough when you first start a job, then lighten up once the trial period passes. A boss can be even tougher if he or she is new in the job and you've been in your position for some time. Be aware of your boss's insecurities. Give your boss time to settle into the position and gain confidence in his or her authority.

An offshoot of this strategy is that you can allow your boss to take credit for your results—once. This might satisfy your supervisor's ego enough so that he or she is ready to give you recognition in the future. But allow this to happen only once; do not let it settle into a pattern. Next time, your boss should be thanking you and giving you the credit. Don't trust an evildoer three times like Snow White did.

Strategy #3. Try to understand your boss's point of view. Sharon G. Hadary, executive director of the Center for Women's Business Research, suggests: "Rather than thinking of this person as an enemy, try to understand why he or she is behaving this way. Perhaps there are ways to help this person achieve his or her own objectives, and in so doing become a respected colleague."

Never confront, challenge, or even try to talk reasonably with your boss *immediately* after the issue arises just because you have something to get off your chest or you want closure. Wait for the strategic moment, when you think she might be more amenable to a productive discussion. During the discussion, listen carefully and completely before relating your point of view. When you have a chance to speak, keep your defensive statements concise and calm. Focus on offering solutions and ways to improve the situation, instead of reiterating your conflicting point of view.

"Through deliberately limiting my defensive response and gutting it out while I collect myself, I am less vulnerable because I rarely overreact on the spot with words I can't retract," says Patty Francy.

If you suspect that your boss is jealous and sees you as a threat, try to muster up some empathy. Maybe your boss was undercut by an employee before and has a reason to be paranoid. Perhaps your boss can clearly see that you could do his or her job better. Maybe your boss is intimidated by your smarts, energy, and ambition. Maybe you can convince her that you're an asset to the team, not a threat. Or maybe your boss will eventually get out of your way and you'll move up the ladder way past him or her.

Strategy #4. Pick your battles carefully. If you're having a difficult time with a boss, assess the situation dispassionately and pick your battles strategically. Sun Tzu summed it up in *The Art of War* over 2,500 years ago when he wrote, "He who knows when to fight and when not to fight will win."

Before you start an overt conflict with your boss, examine your motives. Are you angry? Do you feel a compelling need for justice? Is revenge your motive? These are not solid motivations in the business world. Securing or advancing your career, saving your job, or getting fair compensation and recognition are more valid motivations for a battle.

Even Sun Tzu, who was a ruthless general concerned only with winning, advocated caution and restraint. In *The Art of War* he warned that a battle should never be fought out of anger or resentment. "If not in the interests of the state, do not act," he cautioned. And so it goes in the world of work. If you don't stand to benefit from a confrontation with your boss, do not engage in battle. If you're not in danger, do not fight.

And pick battles that you have a good chance of winning!

Strategy #5. If the situation becomes dire, speak to your mentor, your boss's boss, or to a human resources officer. It is never explained why Snow White doesn't speak to her father about the stepmother's maltreatment. But in the real world, you have to consider all your options to avoid the victim role.

There are some situations in which there is no recourse. Your immediate boss's higher-up may be inaccessible, or entirely in thrall to the person who is giving you trouble. There may be a boss/owner/tyrant rolled into one, and no one else with any authority. In these situations, the first step is to try to change your boss's attitude and win him or her over. If that proves impossible, you need to decide if the advantages of your job outweigh the pain of dealing with your boss, and if you want to tough it out or look for another job.

In many larger companies and organizations, however, there will be someone to whom you can turn. If you have a powerful mentor, this is an ideal person. Otherwise, a human resources officer may be appropriate. Or you may want to speak to your boss's boss.

Strategy #6: Evaluate your options carefully and objectively.

It is always tricky—and risky—to go over your immediate boss's head, but sometimes it is necessary. Asking yourself these questions, and weighing the answers, will help you decide what to do:

Are my boss's complaints and criticisms about me valid? Could my boss convince a higher-up they are valid, even if I don't think they are true? If the complaints can be justified, you're going to have a difficult time making your case.

Have I tried my best to win my boss's approval? Have I given the situation enough time? Give yourself a reasonable period of time—three to six months—to see if you can improve your relationship with your boss.

Is my boss truly abusive, or does he or she just have a negative style? If a boss is abusive, going to human resources or the senior boss may be necessary. But if your difficult boss is merely acerbic, sarcastic, grumpy, or critical, you may be overreacting. Look at the situation objectively to discern if you are being too sensitive. Try to separate the work from your feelings. (This is something that many men do well.)

Is there another position for me in this company if I can't work with my current boss anymore? Before you go to human resources or a higher-up, research whether there is another position in the company that would be suitable for you. Have your résumé and documentation of your current work performance ready. This is where your peers (think Seven Dwarves) can also be helpful. Word spreads, and if your coworkers say you're great to work with, a boss in another department is more likely to welcome you.

Does my boss have a close relationship with the person from whom I seek help? Understand company politics and alliances before making your move. If the boss who's giving you a hard time is chummy with the human resources officer or the senior boss, that doesn't mean you can't speak to them. But you will have to temper your argument. Be sure that you avoid saying anything negative, accusatory, or controversial about your boss. Try to frame the conflict in a nonthreatening way by saying that your styles don't mesh, or that you feel you'd be more productive in a different position.

Strategy #7: Wait for your enemy to self-destruct like the evil queen. Angie was given an assignment in a time of crisis and did not make the best decision. Her boss pointed out her mistake to higher-ups and staunchly voiced that Angie should be fired. A higher-up who was a supporter said, "Just keep working and doing your job because you do it well." Instead of allowing her emotions to rule, Angie kept her cool and continued to do her best. She gained support from her coworkers, who knew that she was a valuable team member and that her mistake was a rare incident. Not long after this incident, the boss who had tried to get Angie fired was let go. In fact, her overreaction to Angie's mistake had damaged her reputation with more level-headed higher-ups. Angie was kept on and continued to work her way up in the company.

In the original Grimm version of *Snow White,* the evil queen goes to Snow White's wedding, where "…she could not stir from the place for anger and terror, for they had ready *red-hot* iron shoes, in which she had to dance until she fell down dead." (Great visual, isn't it?)

Nine times out of ten, this is the fate of people who can't let go of anger and resentment, who are cruel and unfair. They burn their own bridges and self-destruct. They eventually tangle with the wrong person and get what they deserve. So the best strategy is sometimes to wait for the difficult boss to self-destruct or burn out.

Once the dust clears, exercise compassion and forgiveness. It may be hard, but it will work in your own favor. Seeking revenge or holding a grudge can eat you up. Remember: The person who makes you angry controls you. Sometimes you have to let it go, even if a boss was unfair and never acknowledged the mistake or apologized. It never pays to burn your bridges in business.

··

Twenty-First Century *Snow White*

Once upon a time, a talented woman was working as a junior designer in a large clothing company in which there was a constant ferment of gossip and backstabbing. But this kind-hearted woman ignored all the intrigue and treated everyone with respect and kindness. And so she was known as Snow White.

The company was owned by a conglomerate that cared only about the bottom (not hem) line and left everything to the head designer. He took credit for any successful style the company produced, whether it was a knockoff of a Paris original or a new creation by a junior designer. And he kept the myth of his creativity alive by fostering insecurity and envy among his staff, while seducing the owners of the company with impressive sales figures.

One day a fashion reporter wrote an article saying that Snow White, a rising design talent, was creating the most exciting new looks in women's sportswear. Upon reading this piece, the head designer was seized with self-doubt. So he asked the magic mirror (he had a vivid imagination) in his showroom: "Mirror, mirror, on the wall, who's the hottest designer of all?" The mirror replied: "Once you were trendy and hot it's true, but now Snow White is far hotter than you."

The head designer turned pale with envy beneath his winter sun-tan. He summoned the human resources manager and told him to fire Snow White immediately. Then he circulated a story that Snow White was fired for having a drug problem that had spun out of control.

Since the human resources manager knew that Snow White was well-liked among her peers as well as talented, he couldn't bear to fire her without cause. So he transferred her to the company's garment factory in a faraway state, where the head designer would neither see her nor hear of her.

Snow White was lost and terrified by her sudden exile, but a kindly supervisor decided to give her a chance. "If you can cut it as a sample maker, you may stay," he said. "I know it's not as creative as design, but are you willing to work hard anyway?" "With all my heart," Snow White replied. And before too long she had won over the supervisor and her coworkers with her diligence, as well as with her charming habit of whistling while she worked.

Then the fashion reporter decided to do a follow-up story about young designers who burn out quickly. The reporter discovered that Snow White was still employed by the company and used her as a case study in the article. When the head designer read it, he was enraged to learn of Snow White's seamless transition to sample maker.

"This time I will get rid of her for good!" vowed the head designer. He sent Snow White a fruit basket (from a secret admirer), containing apples spiked with an illegal substance. Then he ordered mandatory drug testing of all employees at the production facility. Snow White was fired when her drug testing results came back positive.

When they heard the sad news, Snow White's coworkers gathered in her defense. "We must do something to save her," they cried. The loyalty of the coworkers swayed the supervisor and he took a risk. He gave Snow White a sewing job, off the books. The pay was low and the hours long, but since Snow White was now an undocumented worker, the head designer would not know that she was still employed.

As Snow White sewed, she planned a strategy to revive her career. She decided to contact the fashion reporter who had written the story that ignited the head designer's envy. It happened that in the past this reporter had been the victim of the head designer's diatribes, when she didn't give his collection glowing reviews. And so the reporter was interested to hear Snow White's story and inspired to delve into aspects of the head designer's business practices and management style.

Once the reporter started poking around, a flood of disgruntled former employees, unpaid vendors, and dissatisfied clients came forward with fuel for a juicy exposé. Once it was published, the board of the conglomerate was displeased with the negative publicity, not to mention the implied threat of litigation. They convinced the head designer to step down before he was publicly fired, and his career was in tatters.

Snow White was reinstated as a designer, and now that she was in the press radar her career flourished. When she was named director of design, she started a scholarship program for design students and gave out seven scholarships in the first year. Snow White was known as a benevolent boss (a rarity in the fashion world), and under her direction the company attracted the most talented and dedicated people.

Fairy Dust from *Snow White*

- You are more likely to evoke envy at work because of your ambition, drive, talent, results, and recognition than your looks.
- The wicked queen might be a male or female boss, younger or older, or even a peer.
- Coworkers are important allies. Work in a way that inspires their loyalty and support.
- Whistle while you work—do your job with a good attitude even if you deserve a better position.

- If you have a difficult boss, try to win him or her over with sheer excellence. Always document your efforts and results.
- Strive to understand your adversary's point of view. Pick a strategic time to discuss difficulties.
- Be ready to offer solutions. This is very important!
- Pick the battles you want to fight carefully. Fight to win—not to vent your anger or frustration.
- Sometimes the best strategy is to wait for a difficult boss to mellow out, burn out, or self-destruct.
- Once the dust clears, exercise compassion and move on.

CHAPTER 3

··

Little Red Riding Hood

Stay on the Right Path and You Can Fend Off the Wolf Yourself

LITTLE RED RIDING HOOD IS LURED OFF THE SAFE PATH TO Grandmother's house by a cunning wolf and pretty flowers. Women at work are often waylaid by naiveté, backstabbing coworkers, work overload, and conflicting priorities. The storybook heroine is saved by a huntsman—but in the real world you have to develop your own defenses.

Little Red Riding Hood is a classic cautionary tale that resonates deeply in our collective female psyches. No one can forget the red cloak that symbolizes both sex and violence, and the mounting suspense of the questions between the girl and the wolf at grandmother's house.

Although the story had older roots as an oral tale, it was first published by Charles Perrault in 1697. The story was later adapted by the Grimm Brothers as "Little Red Cap" in their 1812 collection and revised in later editions. Since *Little Red Riding Hood* never made it into the Disney princess pantheon, she is not an icon on the level of Snow White or Cinderella. Yet her humble status makes her closer to all of us—an ordinary girl who must survive trickery and temptation without the intervention of fairies or magic.

Here is the basic story:

*Little Red Riding Hood's mother gives the girl a basket of cakes
to bring to her grandmother, who is ill. On her way through the
woods, the girl meets a wolf. She is so innocent that she doesn't
know he is dangerous, and so they have a pleasant chat. The wolf
distracts her with pretty flowers and diverts her into taking a
roundabout route to her grandmother's house. Meanwhile, he goes
directly to the grandmother's house and tricks her into opening
the door by pretending to be Little Red Riding Hood. Then he
eats up the grandmother and disguises himself in her bedclothes.
When Little Red Riding Hood arrives, he taunts her with tricky
answers until she says: "But grandmother, what big teeth you
have." "The better to eat you with, my dear," says the wolf,
whereupon he springs out of bed and swallows her up.*

Little Red Riding Hood Grows Up

Perrault's version ends badly for the heroine: the wolf eats up Red
Riding Hood and that is the end of it. The witty French author
concludes with a moral that must have evoked knowing winks at
Versailles: "Children, especially well-bred young ladies, should
never talk to strangers, for if they should do so they may well provide dinner for a wolf. I say 'wolf,' but there are various kinds of
wolves. There are those who are charming, quiet, polite and unas-
suming, complacent, and sweet.... And, unfortunately, it is these
gentle wolves who are the most dangerous ones of all."

The Grimm Brothers version has a more upbeat ending: A
huntsman slits open the wolf's belly with his knife, and Red
Riding Hood and her grandmother emerge. Red Riding Hood, no
longer the hapless innocent, takes responsibility for her future
safety when she brings in big stones to fill the wolf's belly so that
he can't recover. And she vows that she will "never wander off into
the forest as long as I live, when my mother forbids it."

These different endings illustrate the two major lessons of
Little Red Riding Hood for working women. First, via the French
tale: don't trust strangers, and learn to recognize wolves in all

their disguises. The German version emphasizes the next lesson: Stay on the path and do not stray from going directly to your destination.

Later adaptations of *Little Red Riding Hood* reflect more female autonomy, as the girl saves *herself*. In Stephen Sondheim's musical *Into the Woods* she overcomes the wolf and then appears wearing a coat made of his fur. In James Thurber's "The Little Girl and the Wolf," Red Riding Hood takes a gun from her basket and shoots him. "It is not so easy to fool little girls nowadays as it used to be," is the tongue-in-cheek moral of the Thurber short story.

Wolves in the Workplace

In the business world, the rescuing figure of huntsman might take the form of a mentor, a boss, or a human resources officer—and may well be a hunts*woman*. But you can't always rely on another person to save your skin.

Every woman in the workplace has to be ready to protect and rescue herself.

When I started the Women On Their Way program—in a traditional Southern-based corporation and in the male-dominated travel industry—it was a controversial move. I had to face skepticism both outside my company and inside. Competitors gleefully predicted that the program would be a money pit. One executive would pass by my office and jokingly say: "She's VP in charge of *skirts*."

This was not the first time I had to deal with wolves in the workplace, nor will it be the last. Every person who sets out to turn her vision into reality will encounter hostile forces. Every woman who has ambition will face detractors. Some opponents will be openly hostile, although they're often the easier ones to dispatch. People who deride or conspire against you behind your back can be even more dangerous.

How to Recognize a Wolf in Sheep's Clothing

- Pay attention to your intuition. Don't dismiss your feelings as paranoia.
- Never assume that everyone means well, even if you do.
- Don't be afraid to recognize both the bad and the good in people.
- If you give someone the benefit of the doubt the first time around, don't ignore the warning signs a second or third time.
- Talk to trusted coworkers or, preferably, associates outside the office, to get their opinion of the person you suspect.

Protecting Yourself and Your Job

When you're attacked, the normal reaction is to turn your own fangs on the person—but this "catfight" response is rarely the best tactic. Fighting back effectively requires less fighting, more patience, and, most of all, strategic thinking. Wolves are cunning, and you need to be, too. Before you act, consider the following tactics. Decide which ones are strategic in your situation and make a plan.

Keep doing your job well, no matter what. This is number one. Having a good base performance to fall back on is crucial. You must find a balance between ignoring an opponent and spending too much time and energy on fighting back. Don't let your worry and countermoves interfere with your first priority: delivering results.

Gain yardage. Defend your position and remain offensive to gain "yardage." This rarely means open aggression or immediate retaliation, especially for women. These reactions only diminish your professionalism and enforce prejudices against ambitious women. Don't fight back just because you are provoked. Choose your response and timing carefully.

Be a political animal. There is nothing wrong with paying attention to office politics. This does not mean you should do anything that compromises your own sense of fairness and inclusion. But remain keenly aware of office alliances, friendships, and rivalries.

Surround yourself with supporters. When the wolf first encounters Little Red Riding Hood, he resists the impulse to eat her right up because there are woodcutters working nearby. The crafty wolf knows he must isolate his prey before he can devour her. In the workplace, too, dangerous people will keep their distance when you have allies around.

Be extra-prepared. Take additional steps to prepare before meetings where you'll face adversaries. Write down your talking points in advance, even if it's an informal meeting. Have profit and revenue numbers ready to prove your points. And always keep a detailed record of your efforts and achievements.

Kill enemies with kindness and laughter. An amused, superior reaction can discourage derision. If someone mocks you, give a big smile and laugh along. But make it clear that you're not laughing at yourself; you're laughing at the other person's immaturity and rudeness.

Talk to your adversary directly. This strategy will only work with certain people at certain times, usually when the conflict is fairly new. If you assess that the detractor is approachable, have a direct but nonaccusatory conversation to scope out his or her feelings. If there is any validity behind the negativity, determine if there is something reasonable you can do to change the other person's attitude.

Put a backstabber on notice that you know you've been attacked. A backstabber is likely to meet your confrontation with denial. But remember, humor is often the best way to diffuse tension. Backstabbers are often passive-aggressive cowards who back down if they know you're onto them.

Speak to your mentor, a trustworthy higher-up boss, or a human resources person. This tactic serves two purposes. You gain practical advice and support, and you make people who count aware of the conflict so they can't be fooled into believing the other side.

Exercise patience. Sometimes just doing your job well and being patient is the answer. The negative person might learn to respect you, or at least lose interest in tearing you down. Another possibility is that the wolf will tangle with the wrong person and blood will spill—but not on you.

Limit your exposure to the detractor. Avoid the person when you can. Walk away from a confrontation. Some people lose interest if you refuse to engage in combat. Look at your options for moving to a different department. If you are in a small company and there is no where to go, start thinking about an exit strategy.

Survive Defeat and Come Back Stronger

The happier ending of *Little Red Riding Hood* symbolizes the potential for rebirth and renewal after defeat. The girl emerges from the wolf's belly, a metaphor for birth. She is chastened and more cautious, but also ready to take responsibility for her own survival.

In many situations, you can defang or escape from a wolf by taking the high road. You can fight back by being smart, clever, and brave instead of nasty. However, there may be times when the enemy wins—temporarily. However, this does not have to be the end of the story. If you keep your integrity and will to persevere intact, you can learn from your mistakes and come back stronger than before.

As women are laid off or fired for not winning at the politics of business, the reflexive reaction is to become bitter and vengeful. "Someone wronged me so it's an eye for an eye, a tooth for a tooth—or at least let me buy a voodoo doll!" While it's natural to feel this way, it's not good for your career or your health in the long run. Pent-up feelings of being wronged or persistent anger can cause marital problems, make you physically ill, and even lead to road rage. At the very least, these emotions drain your energy and productivity. If you can't get past your anger and resentment, it is important to talk to a professional counselor, social worker, or therapist. Feelings are real to you, even if you may be overanalyzing, obsessing, or being too sensitive. Sometimes it is necessary to express your rage in a supportive atmosphere before you can move on.

Sexually Predatory Wolves

When Laura, a recent college graduate, went to work at a midsize corporation, the man who hired her seemed like the nicest guy. Since he was 20 years older and knew that Laura had a serious boyfriend, she didn't guess he had an ulterior motive in his hiring decision. She was genuinely surprised when he made a pass as they were both working late one evening. Then he came on to her again after a business lunch. But since he took "no" for an answer, she didn't tell anyone. And so she was devastated when she found out that people in the office thought she was having an affair with this man.

Luckily, soon after the rumors began to surface, Laura was transferred to another location. It seemed that this guy had a reputation, and one of the top women in the company recommended Laura for a promotion to get her out of his clutches. Nothing was ever said, but Laura was always grateful for the intervention.

In my work lifetime (and I'm in my mid-40s), I've seen a huge shift in the attitude toward sexual harassment in the workplace. I've seen business gossip go from: "You know how *she* got ahead don't you? She's in with the top boss," (and they didn't mean in a mutually respectful business relationship) to: "You know how *she* got ahead? She's smart and got her MBA and is a really great manager."

I've gone from having to accept that a boss could pinch me or speak inappropriately and it was just "part of it" to "Heck no, that's not going to happen."

I know that it's hard for younger women to even believe that businesswomen had to accept a certain amount of shenanigans in the "olden days" that were only 20 years ago. But some men at that time had not fully evolved into accepting women in many industries and positions. I liken it to the old "Monkey Island" at the Memphis Zoo. If I were to fall into the moat surrounding Monkey Island, the monkeys would come and explore and be curious about me. They would poke and prod me to see what I would take and wouldn't take. Some men in the workplace when I entered it were akin to those monkeys. I was new to their territory and they were curious. It was my job to set my boundaries.

When I started my career in Washington, D.C. in the early 1980s, wolves were rampant. And at that time, there was very little you could do except say no, ask a boss for help (if you trusted anyone), and quit if the unwanted sexual advances continued.

Fortunately, the issue of sexual harassment has come out of the closet and is taken seriously. Although this problem has not disappeared, there are established mechanisms for dealing with sexual harassment, especially in larger corporations and agencies.

How to Handle Sexual Harassment
....

1. Make it crystal clear that you do not welcome the person's advances. Don't be ambivalent, coy, or too ladylike. Be firm. Say you respect him or her as a coworker but you have no interest in a fling or a relationship. Be blunt in saying that you do not find him or her attractive. This may put an egotistical person off your scent.
2. Try to avoid situations where you are alone with the person. If he is the only other person who stays in the office late, take your work home instead of hanging around. Your mere presence might encourage unwanted attentions.

(continued)

3. If the unwelcome advances continue, or if any veiled or overt threats are made, tell someone. A senior boss is preferable; if not, a colleague. Don't wait. Tell someone immediately—your best friend, even. In many companies the boss will handle the situation. In other situations the person being harassed needs to go to the human resources department directly.

4. If the person continues to make sexual overtures, consider your options for recourse. This might mean filing a complaint with the human resources officer or getting legal advice. These are big steps and may have repercussions—but do what you need to do to protect your job and yourself.

Stay on the Path of Your Priorities

When Little Red Riding Hood's mother gives her the cake and wine to bring to her grandmother, the mother warns: "Go quickly, before it gets hot. Don't loiter by the way..." Red Riding Hood promises that she will go straight to grandmother's house. But the wolf cunningly diverts her by saying: "Look at the pretty flowers. Why don't you look about you? I don't believe you even hear the birds sing. You are as solemn as if you were going to school." And so Red Riding Hood wanders off among the trees to pick some flowers, and each time she picks one, she sees a prettier one farther on, and goes deeper and deeper into the forest. Meanwhile, the wolf has time to get to the grandmother's house and have her as an appetizer.

Women in the workplace don't need a wolf to lure them off the path. They are sidetracked by conflicting priorities, work overload, unrealistic deadlines, and impossible expectations. And then there is e-mail, paperwork, unnecessary meetings...help!

Picture too many gadgets plugged into too small an outlet—sparks fly and something usually gives out. This is what happens when you're overloaded. My symptoms include flying off the handle when that one last thing, usually petty, just sets me off. And I find myself going back to whomever it was and making an apology.

If you're ambitious and want to get ahead, there is no way to escape overload. You can't fight it or hide from it, unless you want to bury yourself in a dead-end job. Instead, you have to learn to manage work overload and keep functioning at a high level even when you have too much on your plate.

Clarify Your Priorities and Make a Plan

One tool for managing work overload is to set priorities that relate directly to your goals—and then perform or delegate the tasks associated with the priorities.

- The *goal* is where you're headed, the end result you want to achieve.
- The *priority* is the action or person that has the most importance or takes precedence.
- The *task* is the particular piece of work, assignment, or activity.

Priority Planning

Try this simple technique for managing your work day more efficiently. Make a list of your work-related goals divided into these categories:

- Long-term goals (one to five years)
- Mid-term goals (three months to one year)
- Short-term goals (one week to three months)

(continued)

Make another list of your top three priorities at work.

Plan what you'll do each day of the work week on the preceding Thursday or Friday. When you're planning, evaluate each task and see if it:

- Furthers your goals
- Fits in with one of your higher priorities

Avoid Detours

Once you have identified your priorities and planned your day, there's another huge challenge: staying with the plan. Most of us face an avalanche of interruptions on a typical work day. Although distractions can never be eliminated altogether, simple changes in your work style can reduce them to a manageable level.

Don't Get Lost Online

E-mail and Internet browsing save us an enormous amount of time—and they waste an enormous amount of time. Take charge of your online habits or you'll get lost in the woods very fast.

When you're working on a project or task, decide if it's e-mail sensitive. Are you waiting for an e-mail answer or data to complete the job? If not, don't make the mistake of answering your e-mails as they are received. Set yourself a limit—maybe once every two hours, when you'll need a break anyway—and wait until then to check e-mail. Use a Blackberry or PDA and mark "unopened" those e-mails that you need to go back to and answer and/or flag them with a date to return on your computer. Or use the mailbox features in your desktop system to sort and save.

Remember, you don't have to immediately answer all e-mails, especially if you're stressed and tired. Sometimes just waiting a day will put things in perspective.

Keep your e-mails short and to-the-point. It will encourage other people to do the same. Add a "thanks" or "have a good day" to let recipients know that that you're wrapping it up and they don't have to respond.

Pick up the phone sometimes in lieu of sending an e-mail. Explaining yourself verbally can be quicker and better than composing an e-mail. Or make a call if you don't get a response to an e-mail instead of sending more messages. The personal touch, especially for a high-level executive, is a must.

Watch your personal Internet browsing at work. Companies do not appreciate employees wasting time on personal surfing, and some of them can track what you're doing online. Unless it relates to your business, don't have your Internet set up to open on a window of news and diverting features. The idea is to reduce tempting distractions on your computer so you can get right to your priorities.

Streamline Meetings

Meetings eat up a huge part of the workday for most of us. While they are essential, it's very frustrating when they go on too long or are unproductive. Take these steps to streamline meetings:

- Work on items that are important to you before the meeting with others who are attending. Then, when these topics come up in the meeting, you've already resolved offline any major hurdles and you can avoid long, drawn-out discussions and open conflicts.
- Don't get stuck with always being the note-taker. (Do you ever see the men taking minutes of the meeting?) If you do take notes, write down key words and phrases so that if you're called upon or if you're chairing the meeting, you can summarize quickly.
- If you chair a board or committee meeting, brush up on your Robert's Rules of Orders.

- When you chair, keep on the time schedule promised and let people in the meeting have their say without being too loose or lenient. They will respect you if you say: "It is my responsibility to stay on schedule as chair, so that will have to be the last comment."
- If breaks have not been worked into the agenda, pass a note to a colleague and ask for the break together.

Get Out from underneath Paperwork

As paper arrives on your desk, decide what to do with it. Pick one of these five options:

1. Take care of it immediately yourself
2. Set a date to take care of it
3. Delegate someone else to take care of it
4. File it
5. Toss it

Know and respect your personal style when it comes to keeping or tossing. Personally, I'm a pack rat (or an optimist). I can't help thinking: "Maybe this will be useful someday..." If you are the same way, don't fight it—but organize it. Boxing, filing, and organizing your piles will make them less distracting.

You may resist taking time out to sort, throw, and file. Then think about how much time you waste looking for or through papers. And how much more confident and in control you would feel if you were organized.

If you absolutely can't or don't have time to organize, hire someone. The person can be a professional organizer who sets up a system for you or a college student who works under your direction. Just get a warm body in there to get it done.

When it comes to forms, bills, and other paperwork, these tasks also have to get done—somehow. Unless you have assistance, you have to allot time to do it. And if you do paperwork on time, it will save you time. You'll avoid annoying late charges and other complications. Paperwork actually goes faster and is sometimes painless if you "just do it" and don't put it off. Worrying or stewing about a pile of looming paperwork is much worse than acting on it.

Know When to Say "No"

Here's a secret of CEOs that may surprise you: One of the secrets of their success is the ability to say "no."

Carolyn B. Elman, CEO of the American Business Women's Association, says: "What we've found works best is to have an annual plan which we force ourselves to stick to. When we are tempted to add to the plan, we usually put the idea aside to be considered when we develop next year's plan."

Michelle Peluso, CEO of Travelocity, finds that staying on the right path (priorities) is critical. "Keeping a large team focused means your priorities have to filter all the way down to the most junior employee. Be willing to say no to things. When your team comes to you with 'Here are the new things we can do to improve our revenue,' make sure you are asking 'What can we stop doing to keep you focused on these new things?'"

Personal Interruptions

Women tend to have many more personal interruptions than men. We are the ones to make family plans, buy gifts, attend to details of children's lives, organize eldercare…and the list goes on. We're natural multitaskers, and we're approachable, so people assume it is fine to call us in the middle of the afternoon about a personal matter. And most of us can't or don't want to completely shut the personal out of our workday.

A judicious use of time and some rules will let you feel connected, but not constantly distracted. Try these tricks of busy women:

Compartmentalize. "I try to keep a list of personal distractions and address them all at the end of the day," says Carolyn Elman. "This is particularly challenging in times of crisis, be it a son's wedding or a friend's serious problem. What works best for me is to set aside a specific time to deal with these issues and separate them from the rest of the items I need to do on a given day."

Attend to personal matters during a lower-energy time of the day. Do you have a slump after lunch, or in the later morning? The lower ebb of your energy cycle is a good time for phone calls and e-mails that relate to your personal life (and can't wait for the evening). This routine allows you to save your peak concentration and energy periods of the day for more complex and creative work tasks.

Strike a balance. I always want friends and family to know they can call me at work. But they also know that a long personal conversation is usually not possible. I try to listen to what they are calling about to see if it is an urgent issue or not. Then I schedule another time to talk it out.

Let your children understand that your work is important. You always want to be available if your children need to speak with you. Nonetheless you can establish that work is not the time for a lengthy chat. Kids are usually understanding about work parameters *if* you are consistent.

Stay Strong and Healthy

Getting through the days (and nights) when you are anxious and overloaded can both propel you forward and wear you out. Sometimes when you're swept up in pursuing your goals it is difficult to know your limitations—and it can take a toll. When I had my first advisory board meeting, I broke out in hives from head to toe! I got great reviews on the meeting, but physically and emotionally I was a wreck.

Work overload and the resultant stress can lead to health problems such as a heart attack, recurring migraines, back pain, ulcers, or depression. If you're not careful, you can develop a stress-related illness that will stop you in your tracks. No matter how busy you are, it is essential that you allot some time—even a little—to take care of your physical and emotional needs.

I'm sure you know the litany of healthy living by now: drink lots of water, eat smaller portions and healthier foods, and exercise at least three times a week. You've heard it a million times: "But how do I find the time?" Believe it or not, many busy women do find a way. The top level executives who seem the happiest and most relaxed integrate exercise into their lifestyle. One CEO is an avid bike-rider, skier, and "spinner." Golf, swimming, fishing, yoga, and Pilates are some other activities that are popular with high-powered women.

"Oh sure," you might be thinking, "these women probably have a chef, a personal trainer, and a nanny." And maybe they do. But there are easy and low-cost ways to sneak healthy practices into your lifestyle, even if you're a working mom doing double duty.

Six Inexpensive and Easy Ways to Be Healthier
....

1. Drink water frequently at your desk—six cups a day.
2. Eat six small meals a day instead of three big ones; it will keep your energy up.
3. Bring your lunch to work some days—you'll eat less and save money.
4. Organize a lunch-time exercise group at your office.
5. Exercise with your kids if you don't have time to work out on your own. Walk, bike, run, swim, play sports, dance—whatever they like to do, do it with them.
6. Use exercise videos or DVDs if you don't have time to go out to a class. There are workouts for every taste and fitness level.

Give Yourself a Break

I still get nervous before each and every speaking engagement or board meeting. The butterflies in my stomach never go away. But I've discovered a way to get through the anxiety: I give myself— and others—a break now if something isn't perfect.

Self-preservation and a sense of inherent self-worth, no matter how it goes, are essential. You *do not* have to be perfect. The world won't end if you don't get everything done, or don't do everything right. It isn't easy to get to this point if you are ambitious. I struggle with this on a daily basis and I'm still somewhat of a perfectionist. But I've learned to accept mistakes and flaws.

Perhaps we love fairy tales so much because the heroines are always flawed. They make mistakes and missteps but eventually get to grandmother's house or wherever they are going—and survive whatever is waiting there for them.

Red Riding Hood and the Wolf in Sheep's Clothing

Once upon a time there was a midlevel manager named Janice who worked in a large international corporation.

Janice thought it would be considerate to pick up Douglas, her employee, and give him a ride to the airport, since they were both going on the same business trip. She certainly didn't mind putting in the extra miles in her brand new, cherry red convertible. But she was a bit put off when she picked up Douglas and he didn't comment on the car. Maybe it was because he was embarrassed by his dull brown sedan sitting in his driveway. Still, Douglas should have realized that Janice was 15 years older than he and had earned her dream car with hard work.

When they arrived at the business meeting, Douglas made a point of not sitting with Janice during any of the conference sessions. Janice figured that Douglas was just acting like a teenager and trying to assert his independence. She decided to let it slide because he was generally a good employee. In fact, her only complaint about him was that he sometimes distracted her by insisting that they talk about a project that was not on the top burner.

Once they were back in the home office, however, Douglas continued his bizarre behavior. Sometimes when they were in a casual business conversation with others, Douglas would get up and move to make sure he was directly behind Janice. Since Janice did not have a mean bone in her body, she did not realize that Douglas was actually making faces of disapproval, sarcasm, or even disgust while she was talking. She could not imagine that anyone would behave in such a beastly manner.

When a new boss came into the company and asked Janice if she liked Douglas, Janice even said "yes" because she felt duty-bound to support her employee (whom she had hired). Janice believed in taking the high road. Yet as time went on, she had to recognize Douglas for what he was: a wolf in sheep's clothing. Finally, she confronted him.

"What a big tendency you have to distract me from priorities," she said.

"The better to help you multitask," said Douglas with a supercilious grin.

"What a big issue you seem to have with my position of authority," she said.

"The better to help you grow as a team leader," he smirked.

And so it went on, with Douglas feigning innocence and loyalty. It was a disturbing encounter. Janice certainly was glad to drive off in her little red convertible at the end of the day.

Janice was trapped by her tendency to nurture and look for the best in people.

By the time she recognized that he was dangerous, Douglas had cemented his position in the corporation through his job performance and alliances with coworkers and other bosses. So Janice was caught in a tough situation. She had a competent employee, but one who would never be on her team. She was stuck working with Douglas and watching him influence people and advance.

The lesson is a hard one: the wolf can win and eat Little Red Riding Hood up. (Yet there is a reasonably happy ending to this story.)

Although Janice was stuck with the wolf in her company, Douglas was also powerless to get rid of Janice. Since Janice continued to act with integrity and produce great results, she had many supporters. Continuing to believe in herself and focus on her priorities despite Douglas's presence made her stronger.

And she vowed never to allow naiveté to endanger her career again.

Fairy Dust from *Little Red Riding Hood*

- Wolves in disguise can be the most dangerous. Recognize the good *and* the bad in people.
- Do your job well no matter what people are saying about you. Having a good base performance is the best defense against detractors.
- Surround yourself with supporters and the wolf won't be able to devour you.
- Even if you're defeated, you can come back stronger than ever *if* you preserve your integrity and will to persevere.
- There is no way to escape work overload—you must learn to keep functioning well through it.
- Avoid detours and distractions to stay on the path of your priorities.
- Self-preservation and a sense of self-worth are essential—even when you're not perfect.

CHAPTER 4

··

Hansel and Gretel

Find Your Way through the Forest
to a New Job

HANSEL AND GRETEL EVOKES A PRIMAL FEAR: BEING CAST OUT TO DIE by one's own parents, the very people we trust to protect us. In today's work world this translates into the fear of being laid off or fired by the "parent" company, even if we're as innocent as Hansel and Gretel.

Their mother decides that if they don't get rid of the children, the whole family will die of hunger. In business, too, individuals are often sacrificed for the overall economic health or survival of the company. Layoffs, downsizing, and outsourcing are dangers that can send innocent workers out into the woods. And it can happen to the best of us.

Another peril is being laid off or fired with only a few weeks' severance pay. Like Hansel and Gretel, who are given only a measly piece of bread, we might be sent off with only a token bit of nourishment or, in the case of a bankruptcy or business failure, with nothing at all.

At the onset of the story, Gretel is the weaker of the two siblings, turning to her brother for consolation and guidance. But as the story progresses, her character develops. She takes the initiative—with a bold shove of the witch into the oven. Like a woman

65

faced with a career crisis, Gretel discovers her own strength and resourcefulness when she must fight for her own survival.

The story of Hansel and Gretel was first written down by the Brothers Grimm, who collected it from Dortchen Wild, a story-teller who later became Wilhelm Grimm's wife. Their original telling had the children's birth mother wanting to abandon the children, a rarity in fairy tales, which usually hold out the birth mother as a protective figure. Subsequent versions by the Grimms mitigated the cruelty by turning the maternal figure into a step-mother, a more usual villain in fairy tales.

Here is a synopsis of the story:

A very poor woodcutter lives in the forest with his wife and two children, Hansel and Gretel. The wife goads the husband into agreeing to get rid of the children, so that they will no longer have two extra mouths to feed. The first time Hansel and Gretel are abandoned in the woods by their father, they find their way back home with a trail of pebbles. The next time the children are sent away they leave a trail of breadcrumbs, but the birds eat them up.

Lost in the woods, Hansel and Gretel come to a cottage made of bread, with a roof of cake, and sugar windows. An old woman who is really a witch lures them into the house for dinner, although she actually intends to eat them. *The witch imprisons Hansel and fattens him up for four weeks so that he will be a tasty morsel. One morning the witch says they will bake bread, intending to roast Gretel. But the girl manages to shove the witch into the oven instead, and then frees her brother. The pair fills their pockets with pearls and precious stones they find in the witch's treasure chests, and then heads back to their own home. When they come to a body of water with no bridge or boats, Gretel convinces a friendly duck to carry them across. Once the children arrive home, they find that their father is repentant and his wicked wife is dead. With the bounty of gems from the witch's house, their troubles are over.*

At the beginning of the tale, Hansel takes a leadership role, telling his sister time and again, "We shall soon find the way." Yet Gretel turns out to be the one who saves the day and proves to be stronger. Although she starts off in a dependent role, she gains courage and self-reliance in the face of adversity. Her resourcefulness leads her out of danger and ultimately into a better life. And so it often goes when people are faced with unemployment. Many find that what seems to be a catastrophe leads them into a better position.

Scary as it is, being cast out can force you to find new opportunities with greater rewards.

Watch for Signs of Trouble and Plan Ahead

When Hansel and Gretel overhear their parents plotting to abandon them, it gives the children a chance to make a contingency plan. They leave a trail of white pebbles and find their way home—at least for a while.

Being alert to signs of trouble can also buy time in the world of work. Before layoffs, rumors may swirl around the company or negative reports may surface. Before being fired there are often telltale signs: a bad performance review, not meeting sales quotas or revenue goals, having a project axed, or a problematic relationship with an influential boss. Keep your ears and eyes open to these warning signs so that you can take offensive action.

The best way to prepare for the worst is to keep up your contacts. Become involved in professional organizations. Stay in touch with people in other companies. Touch base with recruiters in your field even when you're not yet looking for a new job. Leave yourself a trail of good contacts to whom you might turn if the need arises.

Evaluate your skills and qualifications. Would you require additional training or another degree if you needed to find another job? The additional training or degree that you pursue while you're still working can be an invaluable addition to your résumé if you lose your job. Look into night, weekend, or online courses that you can fit into your schedule. Being proactive about enhancing your job skills can be a career-saver.

Building a contingency fund is important, too. The goal is to have enough money in liquid savings to cover four to six months' worth of bills and living expenses. This can be a tall order in a tough economy where the cost of living keeps going up, but do the best you can. Make the commitment to live less richly for a period, and budget. If you have savings it will greatly reduce the strain of unemployment and allow you to focus your energy on job hunting instead of juggling bills. With adequate savings, you won't be too "hungry." You may be less compelled to accept a position that is not as good as your previous one.

Get Yourself in Good Condition for the Hunt

Marta had been in a high managerial position at a large company for over ten years. It was her first major job and she had given a lot of herself to growing the company, putting in long days and nights. Then she was laid off in a downsizing sweep. Soon after, her husband moved out, saying he "needed his space." She had been the major breadwinner in the family, and she couldn't help feeling that his decision had much to do with her sudden loss of income.

Coping with emotional betrayal at the same time as the job loss was so devastating that Marta didn't have the confidence to immediately begin looking for a new position. She felt entirely adrift, lost in the woods with nowhere to go. She lost interest in everything, even eating, and became gaunt and lethargic.

Fortunately, Marta had enough savings to take a few months to regroup. She began to volunteer for the animal rescue center so she would have a place to go and do something she believed in. She also reached out to her family, whom she hadn't had much time to see during the last whirlwind decade of work. After finding solace in these nourishing activities, Marta was ready to address her health issues. She went to a nutritionist, who diagnosed her as anemic, and put her on a food and supplement program that helped tremendously. Soon she felt strong enough to go on a whitewater rafting trip to Montana, something she had always wanted to do. Marta regained her confidence to the degree that she could begin to network at social and professional gatherings. She began to get job leads, and before long she found fulfilling work.

Losing a job is stressful, demoralizing, even traumatic. Yet it can also be a wake-up call. Many of us are running so fast that we don't realize we're letting ourselves get run down. When you're stopped in your tracks, the physical symptoms emerge—or the shock of the job loss itself can lead to health problems.

Depression, weight gain or loss, anemia, an underactive thyroid, and other conditions can drain you of the stamina needed for the process of job hunting. So no matter how anxious you are to line up another position, it is wise to take stock of your health before you start a serious job hunt. If you need to get professional help for any emotional or physical maladies, do not procrastinate. Think of it as your first step toward getting your career back on track.

Stay Confident and Optimistic

In the beginning of Hansel and Gretel's saga, Hansel is the one who is optimistic, telling his little sister time and again: "We shall soon find a way." But once her brother is imprisoned by the witch and Gretel realizes that she must rely on her own ingenuity, she gains confidence and ends up taking the lead. Through adversity she discovers the depth of her own courage and resilience.

Staying optimistic and confident during a period of unemployment requires a lot of hope and faith. It is not easy—but it is a prerequisite to success. No one is going to hire you for a great job just because they feel sorry for you. You have to be self-assured and upbeat. This may require remaining hopeful in the face of rejection, blind leads, and disappointments. It's not easy and you'll have to make a systematic effort to maintain a positive outlook.

Five Precious Pebbles:
Ways to Keep Your Spirits Up and Find Your Way Back

1. As you're polishing and adapting your résumé, use it to remind yourself of all your skills and accomplishments.
2. Stay in close contact with supportive friends and family members. Get in touch with old friends and relatives whom you haven't had time to see in a while.
3. Exercise as often as possible. Aim for at least three times a week.
4. Look for volunteer opportunities. Volunteering for a good cause will reinforce your own sense of self-worth as you help others. It can also lead to useful networking contacts.
5. Make time to do activities that nurture your spirit, whether that means communing with nature, visiting art museums, or walking your dog.

My sister, Mary Kenner, is a real inspiration when it comes to remaining optimistic. She was laid off from a big corporation and as a single mom the pressure was intense, yet she always maintained a positive attitude. Mary didn't feel sorry for herself or want anyone else's pity, and she never put herself down in conversations with me or anyone else. She kept her self-image and her ego intact. This gave her the confidence to pull out all the stops when it came to networking. Mary had no qualms about calling any and all contacts she had—even calling on the CEOs of top companies to get in the door at the top. People were impressed not only by her résumé, but by her courage. She clearly showed that she had the right stuff for a high-level position, and she landed one.

Master Job Search Skills

If you are laid off or fired, don't fall into the trap of thinking of yourself as "unemployed." You *have* an important new job: marketing and selling yourself. Take it as seriously as any other job.

Set up regular hours to work at your new business of job hunting. Get up at your usual workday hour and get dressed in a reasonably nice outfit (dress-down Friday wear is fine unless you're going on an interview). If you get a callback, you'll feel more confident talking about your skills if you're wearing presentable clothes than if you're slumping around in your old bathrobe!

Go to your new "office," whether that means the outplacement office, the desk in your basement, or the computer in your living room. Put in at least half a day every day, or better yet, work at your job search full-time, but don't wear yourself down.

Hansel and Gretel found pearls and precious stones in the old witch's cottage. You might find your treasure someplace just as unexpected. You have to explore every avenue, be open to all the possibilities—and keep track of them.

When you first start job hunting your mind will run in a hundred different directions. In addition to your own ideas, you'll have this colleague telling you to call so-and-so and this friend telling you to write to so-and-so. Staying organized is essential. Just as you would at any job, you need to plan your activities, follow-up conscientiously, and document results.

There are many different systems for organizing your job search. You can use index cards, a Rolodex, a PDA, a computer program, or simply a pen and paper. It doesn't matter what tools you use, provided you have a system that you can maintain.

Here is a simple system you can use—or feel free to invent your own.

Job Hunt Organizer
....

Set up a notebook or computer file to keep a running log of your contacts and results. You'll also need a calendar with a full page per day for listing follow-up calls and appointments. Write down:

Who: Name of person you are going to contact along with the phone number, e-mail, and mailing address.

Why: Follow-up on ad, job lead, referral, general advice, or networking

How: Call, e-mail note, e-mail note and résumé, deliver material by hand, or mail

When: Set a date to initiate contact and put it on your calendar.

Action: Write down each call, letter, and message left for the contact.

Result: Note any responses. If the person gave you a new lead, start a new notation for that contact. If you had no answer, or someone told you to call back at a certain time, pick a date to follow up and put it on your calendar.

The Résumé That Gets Results

Your résumé must be more than a laundry list of your previous jobs. It must send a message, or, in PR terms—make a pitch and *sell you* to the employer.

Julie Jarrett, who is a senior associate with the top executive search firm Heyman Associates, has this advice: "Use a chronological format for your résumé with an easily scannable, 11- or 12-point font size. An unusual font will not get you noticed— it's the information on your résumé that counts. It's perfectly acceptable to go more than one page or even two. No one wants to mull through a six-page résumé, but do lay out your accomplishments. If you have more than five years' work experience, don't use an objective; instead, adopt a summary paragraph. Use dates. And it's fine to add a "personal" section—which so many people steer away from. A woman once sent me a résumé and indicated she had an affinity for tennis. When the USTA (United States Tennis Association) came to us with a search, I thought of her immediately because that information stuck with me."

Résumé Checklist
....

- Use a traditional format: Name and contact information at the top; summary; review of jobs and employers, starting with the most recent position.
- Use good-quality paper and have someone else proofread for you.
- List the responsibilities of your former positions, not just titles.
- Highlight major or measurable accomplishments in each job, but keep it concise.
- Customize your résumé for each job application.
- Reflect the skills and qualities that are mentioned in the ad or job description.
- Keep it honest.

The Art of Cover Notes

Whether you send your résumé via the Internet, fax, or mail, you'll need a carefully worded cover note. Keep the cover note brief, but use it as an opportunity to convey some of your personality and special qualities. And check it carefully to make sure there are no typos, since it creates that crucial first impression.

"Recruiters are inundated with résumé volume," says Diana M. Meisenhelter, principal of Riviera Advisors. "So don't be surprised that very few people read cover letters. If you send one, keep it simple and address the major areas: why you are looking for a job, names of people who may have referred you to the company, the position you are interested in, and how to contact you. Focus your time on creating a world-class résumé and getting on the phone and networking."

If you really want the job, don't just send your cover note and résumé into cyberspace and wait for something to happen. Follow up with a "thank you" e-mail or practice the almost-lost art of handwriting a personal note. A note on a fine Crane's or Strathmore card can catch someone's attention.

Know Where to Look

Hansel and Gretel tried three methods to get back home: dropping white pebbles, strewing a trail of breadcrumbs, and finding their own route back by sheer instinct. In job searching terms, you also have three avenues:

Work with outplacement and executive search professionals. Like the trail of white pebbles, this is a smart and effective way to find your direction. If you are offered outplacement services by your company, take advantage of them. If not, research executive search firms or "headhunters" in your field. Working with an expert can give you valuable guidance and access to higher-level jobs that are not publicly posted.

"One should get to know specialty recruiters in one's area/industry of expertise and build that relationship just as you would with your network in general," says Susan Abrahamson, president of Searchcom, Inc., a national executive search firm. "Recruiters are a fount of great info." She also points out that you should treat a meeting with a recruiter as a serious interview, requiring business attire and professional demeanor.

Proactively target companies where you'd like to work. Instead of only going after the pool of advertised or available positions, you can also target desirable companies and strategize on how to find a way in. First, think about what kind of company and position could be a step toward fulfilling some of your long-term career goals. Next, research companies or organizations you find appealing because of proximity, specialty, culture, or another feature. Make a list of these companies and find out whom to contact within the organization. Sometimes this is a hiring manager but occasionally going straight to the top—the president or CEO—yields a response.

Pursue classified ads in newspapers and online. Like Hansel and Gretel's breadcrumbs, this is iffy. The jobs that are advertised might be devoured by the other hungry creatures in the forest before you get a bite.

Still, it can be worthwhile to check published advertisements, especially if you're seeking an entry- or mid-level position. A survey by Bernard Haldane, the career management firm, found that 16 percent of respondents had landed their positions through newspaper advertisements—not a huge percentage but a reasonable return.

It may surprise you to learn that online searches yield less than print ads. A study by Drake Beam Morin, a workplace consulting firm, found that only 5 percent of the people 21 to 37 who were surveyed said they had found jobs through Web sites. And older workers had even less success: only 1 percent of workers 57 and older found jobs online.

It's all too easy and comfortable to sit back in your chair and send your résumé into cyberspace. It looks like a sweet way to find a job but it can leave you empty. Internet searches are fine as one tool among many. But you are competing against thousands for any decent job that is advertised online and it's very hard to stand out. The consensus among employment experts is that Web searches are limited. Networking and active job searching yield the most results.

Active job seeking means good old-fashioned legwork: Make phone calls to people you know and find out who *they* know. Contact companies you're interested in, and go to professional functions and social events. Get out there as much as you can with the personal connection that makes all the difference.

Productive Networking

Networking is not a trend, it is not a catch phrase—it is *the number one* proven tactic for finding rewarding work. A major survey conducted by Bernard Haldane found that 61 percent of people had found their last job through networking and referrals. Other outplacement experts put the number as high as 80 percent.

Are you reluctant to put yourself out there and network? It's natural. We all have to struggle with those feelings of being shy, inadequate, or awkward. Sometimes when you're at a networking event you can feel like you're right back in junior high, standing against the wall waiting for a boy to ask you to dance. But here's the good news: Girls don't wait to be asked to dance anymore. And they don't have to be rescued.

Gretel starts out helpless, but when push comes to shove she outsmarts that witch, fills her apron up with treasure, and leads the way home. And so can you. Take the plunge. Start off networking with people and groups with whom you feel comfortable and then stretch yourself.

Start Close to Home

If you're nervous about networking, ease into it with people you know. Reconnect with old and newer friends, relatives, neighbors, and former coworkers. Get to know acquaintances from your community, alumni schools, religious affiliations—anyone with whom you have a built-in connection.

If you have kids, you probably spend a lot of time taking them to sports activities, lessons, playgrounds, and so on. These places offer good opportunities to talk to other parents, who have other friends and contacts. Who knows where it can lead? People can find valuable networking contacts at daycare, PTA meetings, ballet lessons, or baseball games.

You'll be more comfortable networking if you have a project to talk about that shows you're busy and energetic, not sitting at home feeling sorry for yourself. This is where volunteerism comes in. Think how much better you'll feel about discussing your situation if you can say, "I'm looking for an accounting job but meanwhile I'm volunteering at the senior citizen's center, helping them put a new accounting system in place." Or: "I'm looking for something in fundraising, but while I have the time I'm archiving the museum's donor list."

Volunteer for Good Causes

One surefire way to jumpstart your networking is to *offer* help, instead of just asking for it. Volunteer at your church or synagogue, or answer the phones at a PBS telethon or your school alumni phone bank. The chair of the fundraising committee will notice you and may be able to do you a favor in return. Plus, you never know who you will meet on the phone!

Join in a walkathon to fight breast cancer or heart disease. Volunteering for outdoor events, such as fairs in your local parks to raise money for libraries, firefighters, etc., is also a great way to meet people. When you network by volunteering, you can't lose. Even if you don't meet anyone who offers any professional leads, you'll get a lift from doing some good.

Participate in Professional Groups

Research professional groups that relate to your industry, location, gender, or special skills, then join up and *participate*. The key to making these groups work for you is to work for them. You must show initiative and take an active role. Volunteer for a committee, put in your time, and stay involved—otherwise no one will know that you exist. Show that you're willing to go the extra mile, and people who are in a position to hire or give a referral will take notice.

Attend Events and Conferences

There is no substitute for getting out there and meeting new people. Attend programs that appeal to you within and outside of your industry, since both offer opportunities to learn something new as you expand your network. But to make these activities fruitful, you have to know how to "work the room."

Cindy Burrell, owner of Burrell-Laurent company and Vice President, Corporate Relations for Boardroom Bound,® offers this advice about networking at events: "You do not need to meet everyone. More important is to explain in a concise way what you are looking for and ask for referrals that can get you closer to your goal. The more specific you are, the better results you will have."

Lisa Tromba, principal of executive search at A.T. Kearny, says "Networking is about building relationships and the best way to do that is by helping others. Share knowledge that might benefit and help the other person. Make connections. Find out as much as you can about the other person and tell your story. Most importantly, establish credibility and build the relationship."

It can be a delicate dance to make yourself known at events and conferences without appearing pushy or desperate. Julie Jarrett has some pointers about networking etiquette. "If you're networking at a gathering, ask for a business card and request permission to send an e-mail. In general, people want to help other people network and end up in a good job. If they think they can help, people will offer their hand. If they don't offer, leave the situation alone. If it feels inappropriate, it probably is."

A warning to the wise: Remember how starving Hansel and Gretel were tricked by the sweet temptation of the witch's edible cottage? Beware of high-priced seminars and videos that exploit people who are unemployed. Anything that promises to tell you how to get rich quick—but only after you part with a substantial amount of your money—is probably a scam. I've never heard of these shortcuts being a substitute for hard and smart work.

Make Your Networking Calls Count

If you're making the initial contact via phone instead of in person, you'll have to work even harder to establish rapport. "If you are calling someone to network, leave details in a voicemail. Don't just leave a name and number," suggests Julie Jarrett. "Start with 'I was hoping you could help me network with John Doe at XYZ Company. I believe you have a relationship with him and I understand he is hiring a manager of events.' Don't go on to explain how you would be a perfect fit for the role. Keep it simple but be clear on what you're requesting."

Excel at Interviews

After Hansel and Gretel manage to vanquish the witch and fill their pockets with treasure, they still face one more trial before they find their way back home: crossing a body of water without a boat. In the course of your job hunt, this final hurdle is the interview. It will sink you or land you where you want to go.

First Impressions Count

Most people form their basic opinion of you within minutes of meeting you. You have to make the minutes count, so...

Be on time. *Never* take a chance on being late to an interview. Leave yourself tons of extra time to get there. Then go to a nearby coffee shop and wait. Go up to the office about ten minutes before the interview is scheduled.

Choose your outfit intelligently. If you're not sure what is appropriate for this particular workplace, err on the side of classic and classy. "Research the company's culture," says Julie Jarrett. "Make sure you investigate how employees dress and then 'one up' that level when going to the interview."

People understand if you're dressed a little more formally than you need to be, but no one will be impressed if you look too casual. Always pick out your outfit a few days before and make sure it is pressed, no stains or cat hair, with hose and polished shoes to match.

Prep your answers. Cindy Burrell offered these innovative ways to prepare for an interview: "List your strengths before an interview; then star (*) the strengths that are most applicable to the specific job that you are interviewing for. Next to the starred strengths, jot down specific stories that illustrate each strength. For example, everyone can say that they are persistent—but what makes that statement credible is a story about where your persistence led to success—and *that* is what will be remembered by the interviewer."

Calm yourself—and the interviewer. "Another calming trick is actually used by professional speakers," says Cindy Burrell. "Before the interview, go to the restroom. Drink a glass of water; run warm water over your hands if it's cold outside; take a number of deep breaths, and smile in the mirror. Your body will be ready to support you." Once you're sitting across from the interviewer: "Pretend that the interviewer is a guest in your home, and that you are the perfect hostess making him/her feel comfortable. It's basically a psychological game with yourself—and it works!

It's especially good when the interviewer is being so serious and doesn't crack a smile. Your job is to put the interviewer at ease, build rapport, and make that smile happen!"

During the interview, "Be organized, prepared, and concise. Be focused and don't ramble. Understand that the time frame of most initial and early-stage interviews is one hour," says Nancy Keene, director in the retained executive search firm of Stanton Chase International. "Be sure you have the time, and appropriate timing, to ask the questions you have prepared. And most importantly you want to spell out the three to four most compelling reasons why you are a fit and the best person for a job. Also, *listen carefully.* Don't tell someone how to make the watch if they're only asking you the time."

Interview Success List
....

- Be aware of your body language. An alert but natural and relaxed posture is best. You can cross your legs but never cross your arms.
- Maintain good eye contact.
- Smile and laugh appropriately, but don't giggle too much, since it can be a sign of nervousness, diluting your authority.
- Listen to the questions. Don't jump in with your answers too soon. Keep your answers short and to the point; don't reiterate or drone on.
- Be ready to explain why you left your last job (or were asked to leave) in an honest but tactful manner. *Never* badmouth a former employer.
- Don't compare your past jobs to how the interviewing company operates.
- Act like you definitely want the job—even if you're not sure. You can always decline an offer later if you have second thoughts or find something better.

What Are Employers Looking For?

A certain set of skills is required for every job. But what if you and 500 other people have those same skills, sufficient experience, and good references? What are the special characteristics that will enable you to stand out from the crowd of other qualified applicants?

When I'm hiring, I look for a person who:

- Is well-spoken, smart, and confident
- Is honest, forthright, and able to look me in the eye when we talk
- Can interact with all levels of the organization from the line employees to the CEO
- Will work well with a team, and will fill a matrix of skill sets
- Will fit into the existing company culture but also add something or change it for the better
- Has a spark—something special to bring to the organization that usually comes across as sincerity

When men are being considered for a job they are often looked at for their potential. For women it's more important than ever to see the potential in ourselves because we are often seen first for our limitations. Yes, in many companies, especially in the upper levels, there is still not an even playing field. Women have to shine in job interviews and put their skill and potential right up front so that they can't be ignored.

This might mean taking the plunge and believing you can do something you've never done before. Express willingness to take a risk and take charge. If you show hesitation and equivocate, you can bet your résumé will be shoved to the bottom of the pile. Honesty about your experience is fine, but you must be willing to take on any new challenges the job holds out. What is the worst that can happen?

You might not be perfect; you might fail, but as Judy Carr, an LPGA golf professional once told me, golf is a series of errors and the lesser ones are how you win the game. And if your game falls apart, "Get a check-up from the neck up!" In other words, golf, like business, is a mental game—all in your head—so shake it off if you make an error.

Just think about how women become first-time mothers with no previous experience. They want to do it, they picture themselves doing it, and somehow it works. Taking on a new job responsibility is nothing compared to that! But the only way you'll have a chance to prove you can do it is to exhibit self-assurance in that interview.

Believe it or not, employers are nervous, too. When I hire someone, I consider it a privilege and also a huge responsibility. The person I hire has the potential to make or break my career.

So please remember that the person hiring on the other side of the desk may be just as uncertain and anxious as you. It is your responsibility to give that person absolute confidence in your abilities.

··

Hans and Greta in the New Economy

Once upon a time, two software programmers who had gone to college together went to work for a start-up Internet company. Hans and Greta were excited to be given stock in the company and work in a trendy loft office with ergonomic furniture. The company was overextended and its stock overvalued, but hopes were high.

Then a dot-com crash came upon the land. And Greta overheard the CFO saying to the president of the company: "We've got to downsize. Cut the fat. Get rid of at least 25 percent of the staff."

Greta was terrified, but Hans had an idea. "We'll make ourselves indispensable," he said. "We'll work 12 hours a day instead of 10." And so they did, and they survived the first round of layoffs.

Then one dark day the CFO announced that Hans and Greta were being laid off for "productivity issues." Greta tried to save her job by pleading with the president, but he said, reluctantly, he must follow the CFO's plan. Hansel and Greta had to pack up and vacate the office immediately, with only the promise of a meager two-week severance check in the mail.

"Don't worry," said Hans, as they discussed their dilemma over pricey double lattés at their favorite coffee bar. "We still have our stock in the start-up." But as the weeks went by they found out the stock was worthless. The company was going into bankruptcy and numerous creditors were poised to gobble up whatever crumbs were left.

Fully indoctrinated in the wonders of the Web, Hans and Greta believed they would find new jobs online. Every day they spent hours surfing job sites and e-mailing résumés, but too many programmers were looking for work and nothing panned out. Soon, when Hans and Greta met at the coffee bar to exchange leads, they were reduced to nursing small cups of regular Joe instead of indulging in pricey foam.

Then one day Hans didn't show up for their usual coffee date. With a pile of unpaid bills and no prospects, he had fallen into a depression and couldn't bring himself to leave the house. His optimism evaporated and he felt hopeless. "I'm trapped. I'll never get out of this hole," he lamented to Greta.

Greta realized that she had to take the reins, since Hans certainly wasn't going to come up with any fresh leads in this sorry state. Greta had always been shy about networking, being an introverted type who felt more comfortable behind a screen. But her hunger drove her to action. She started by contacting some of her old college friends. She met them for lunches, gathered leads, and went to see hiring managers at some companies. Finally, she took the plunge and went to a conference for women in technology. There she got referrals that led to not one but two different viable job offers.

Just as Greta was weighing these options, the president of their old start-up called. He said the CFO was gone, the company was reorganizing, and he wanted Hans and Greta back. Hans was inclined to take the offer, since his job-search had yielded nothing and his self-esteem was low. But Greta was feeling her power. And she was not going to bring her resources back to that smarmy former employer—who still owed her the two-week's severance pay!

Instead, she decided to accept the job offer that promised the most stability and offered real benefits instead of crummy stock. Greta told Hans that if he moved quickly, he might find work with the same firm, since she could put in a word with the hiring manager. Hans was so bowled over by how decisive Greta had become that he decided to follow her lead.

And so they both found work at a company that seemed to be solid, although in the new economy, no one could say it would be forever.

··

Fairy Dust from *Hansel and Gretel*

- Take offensive steps if your job is in jeopardy: Save money, further your education, and keep up your contacts.
- Address your physical and emotional health issues to get in condition for the rigors of job hunting.
- Treat your job search like a new job: Market and sell yourself.
- Don't get lost in the woods of Web job searches that lead nowhere. There is no substitute for active job seeking and making personal contacts.
- Look at networking as an opportunity to give as well as to receive. Think about what you can do to help other people, causes, and organizations.
- Give the interviewer absolute confidence in your abilities. Express willingness to take risks and accept challenges.
- Remember that being cast out of your company can lead you to new opportunities with greater rewards.

···

CHAPTER 5

The Ugly Duckling

Paddle Your Way into a Group That Recognizes Your Strengths

LIKE THE UGLY DUCKLING, IN THE TALE BY THE SAME NAME, WOMEN in business are often outcast, excluded, and ridiculed by the brood. We may face derision for daring to fly high and pursue a serious, high-powered career. All too often, we're not recognized as "swans" where we work—and we often fail to recognize our finer qualities ourselves. It takes us a lot of exploring, pushing outside our comfortable boundaries, and even suffering before we find out where we belong. And to achieve our potential we have to find support among those who recognize our talent and strength.

The Ugly Duckling is a literary creation, rather than a written version of an old oral fairy tale. Published in 1844 by the Danish author Hans Christian Andersen, it is one of the most beloved of his 156 tales. The story strikes a deep chord in readers because Andersen uses the anthropomorphized duck to convey his own experience of being an outsider struggling to find his place in the world.

Although Hans Christian Andersen became a celebrated author, he was born into abject poverty, the son of a shoemaker and a washerwoman. As a highly emotional child, he was ridiculed by his peers because of his sensitivity, effeminate interests, and gawky appearance. At age 11, Andersen's father died and the boy was forced to apprentice in a series of jobs for which he was ill-suited. No one recognized his worth until he moved to Copenhagen at age 14 to pursue a career as a singer, dancer, and actor. In the artistic atmosphere of the city he found supporters, even a mentor who gave him a grant to enter grammar school and later university. But he ultimately failed as a performer and nearly starved to death. It wasn't until he focused his creativity on writing that he found his forte. Andersen wrote plays, novels, poems, and travel books, but it was his successive volumes of *Fairy Tales and Stories,* published between 1835 and 1872, which brought him lasting acclaim.

Andersen's telling of *The Ugly Duckling* is beautifully poetic, with layers of meaning that you may not have absorbed as a child. Reread this tale and other classic Andersen stories and you'll be surprised at how much they have to offer adults. Meanwhile, here is a summary of the story of *The Ugly Duckling,* that plucky creature with a lot to teach us all.

> *A duckling is born looking different than the rest of his brood: bigger, ungainly, and gray. The other ducklings relentlessly tease and torment him for being different. Even his mother, who had faith that he would shape up, becomes so exasperated that she wishes he would go away. And so the Ugly Duckling flies away from his brood and joins a group of wild geese, but they are caught in the crossfire of a shooting party. Next the Ugly Duckling finds refuge in an old woman's cottage, but the cat and hen who live there look down upon the duck and his penchant for swimming. Painfully missing the freedom of floating on the water, the duckling goes back to the wild. He sights a flock of beautiful white birds, but doesn't dare to dream that he might be accepted by these magnificent creatures.*
>
> *The Ugly Duckling suffers through a long, lonely winter with many hardships, including being trapped by ice and nearly pummeled by a peasant woman. But once spring*

comes, he raises his wings and finds himself stronger than ever before. He flies off to a lovely garden at the shores of a lake, where he meets up with three beautiful swans. There, in the water, he sees in his own reflection that he, too, is a majestic swan. The other swans swim round him, stroking him with their bills, and little children in the garden call out to him with delight. He rustles his feathers and raises his head to the sun, filled with more happiness than he ever dreamed possible.

Recognize the "Swan" in Your Own Reflection

The Ugly Duckling must recognize his own beauty and majesty before he can find acceptance and appreciation in the world at large. And women must be secure in their own sense of worth before they can attain the recognition and reward they deserve at work. This doesn't come easily, since women sometimes are their own worst critics, focusing on their shortcomings instead of their talents. Men in business, however, tend to do the opposite—they trumpet their strengths and hide or brush aside their weaknesses.

Some women come into the workplace brimming with self-assurance, fully hatched right into swanhood. However, many others (like myself), have to consciously work at strengthening their self-image. This is not necessarily a negative. Some of the most ambitious and successful women in the world have fought a long and never-decisive battle with insecurity.

The need to prove yourself can actually kindle drive and ambition. You don't have to grow up feeling or looking like a swan to become one.

People might assume when they see me on a television talk show or giving a speech in front of three hundred people that I'm naturally extroverted and confident. But as a woman in business I've often felt like an Ugly Duckling and it has—and still does—take a concentrated effort of will to keep my feathers fluffed and my neck tall as a swan.

There is no magic recipe for self-confidence or self-esteem. But here are a few tricks of the trade that I've found helpful.

Identify Your Own Strengths

The first and foremost way to recognize your value is to realize that you are not perfect, not infallible, not good at everything—but you *are* very skilled and talented at some things. You will accomplish some of your goals and not others, and that's okay. Your successes will show you what you're good at and your failures will show what you're not meant to be or do.

Hans Christian Andersen failed as a performer but became a celebrated author. His alter-ego, the Ugly Duckling, failed as a duck, a goose, and a household pet, but made it as a swan. And every successful woman has endured her share of failures, and will admit that there are still certain things she's not good at.

No one is good at everything. The secret is to identify your talents and skills, cultivate them, find a job where you can use them, and find people who appreciate what you can do.

Duckling to Swan Exercise
•••••••••••••••••••••••••••••••••••••

Write down:

- What you are good at that you do now.
- What you are good at that you don't have enough opportunity to do in your current job.
- What steps you can take to have more opportunity to use your skills and talents at work.
- Memorable instances when you accomplished something special in your career.
- Occasions when you were recognized with a promotion, raise, bonus, or award.

(continued)

- Three steps you can take to get more recognition at work right now.
- Three steps you can take to get more reward in the future.

Give Yourself a Pat on the Back

As a public relations and marketing professional, I've always been good at letting the world know how wonderful my client or company is, yet I've been reticent about blowing my own horn. I would depend on other people to tell me I'm good at what I do, and waiting for these crumbs of praise to fall my way was draining. Eventually I learned that people who are happy in their work know how to give themselves a pat on the back and say "Job well done," even before anyone else does.

Once you're comfortable giving yourself private congratulations, you can learn to let others know about your accomplishments. You don't have to be an outrageous egotist trumpeting your superiority to the world at large. But you have to be ready to let people know what you're good at *and* make it clear that you understand your own value and your gifts.

Five Steps to Tasteful Self-Promotion

1. Informally let coworkers and bosses know about your results.
2. When appropriate, circulate memos, reports, or letters from clients complimenting your work.
3. Offer to give presentations at meetings.
4. Contribute articles to the company newsletter or industry newsletters.
5. Get quoted in industry publications and newsletters (check to see if this requires company approval).

Don't Be Too Demure

When you communicate assertively, you will have a better self-image and gain more respect and esteem from others. Connie Glaser, author and consultant on women's workplace issues, finds that "Because of our social conditioning and learned 'ladylike' behavior, women often have to unlearn the submissive communication habits we picked up as children. One of women's greatest issues in the workplace is being taken seriously, particularly by men. Yet sometimes women will inadvertently sabotage themselves by using certain speech mannerisms that rob them of their credibility, such as excessive apologies, hedges, saying 'kinda, sorta, like…you may this think is a stupid question, but….' We also have to watch out for giving too many details and taking too long to get to a point. Women need to be able to ask for what they want succinctly, directly, and confidently."

Don't Confuse Humor and Humiliation

Growing up in the deep South in the "olden days" just before the Women's Lib movement, I internalized the idea that nice girls have to hide behind a dainty demeanor of modesty—or self-deprecating humor.

For instance when a company I was working for was going through a period of layoffs, I said, "Well, they probably won't lay me off since I'm not making enough to be costing the company much money." As soon as I said it I knew it was a mistake to denigrate my salary and my importance to the company, while also making light of the serious matter of layoffs.

Making jokes at our own expense is a habit you may find in many more women in business than men. Maybe we feel we have to make fun of ourselves before someone else does it for us. But self-deprecating humor falls flat in the work world. It devalues your currency and weakens your image in the eyes of others, as well as yourself. It's fine to be funny—I think humor is priceless in the workplace—but be sure the jokes aren't at your own expense and that you're not using humor in a way that demeans you.

Accept That Not Everyone Will Be a Supporter

Many women equate being *liked* with being *good*. And so they end up feeling like the Ugly Duckling, who couldn't find acceptance among the ducks, the geese, or the old woman's menagerie, no matter how hard he tried to fit in.

If you want to survive in the wilds of the business world, it's crucial to accept that you just won't click with some people. Being nice, honest, and a team player isn't always enough. Some people won't like you no matter what you do—and that's okay.

Jane, a midlevel manager in a large corporation, always prided herself on being friendly, fair, and considerate. So when her boss told her that there were several people in her department who didn't like her, she was surprised and hurt. However, after a great deal of thought and worry about this situation, Jane decided *not* to directly confront the people who supposedly didn't like her. Since they were not behaving in a hostile or even uncooperative manner, it didn't seem appropriate to put them on the spot. She also decided against offering them an apology, since she hadn't done anything wrong. Instead, she determined to try extra hard to watch her behavior and word choices with those particular people her boss had named.

One person at a time, she made an effort to do a special favor, take the person out to lunch, or provide some extra help on a project. It was a conciliatory but subtle strategy that didn't compromise her pride or authority. And a most important component of the strategy was for Jane to acknowledge to herself that not every one of these people was going to become a big fan.

Over time her efforts yielded results. Some of these coworkers became much more engaged and friendly, stopping by her office to chat, giving her welcome advice and information. There remained some people whose attitude toward her was hard to decipher, but even these colleagues clearly respected Jane. And she gained a new level of self-assurance because she was able to live with the fact that she was not always going to be Miss Popularity.

Here's how to handle coworkers who don't like you and may be cold or distant, which makes working together a strain.

- A direct confrontation can sometimes make matters worse and is not called for if the person is working with you cooperatively.
- Helping people with their projects and being a team player is the best way to win them over.
- Sometimes personalities don't mesh and there's little you can do except be cordial and professional.
- If people don't like you, they may be motivated by envy or insecurity. Take it as a compliment.
- Sometimes you and the people in your workplace are under such pressure, with little sleep, that everyone is stressed and irritable. It has nothing to do with you. Keep yourself rested and don't take comments personally.

Understand the Family Factor

The Ugly Duckling's mother tries to train him to walk duck-footed with his toes turned out and quack at appropriate intervals so he can fit in with the brood. Nonetheless, the Ugly Duckling is relentlessly teased, chased, and bitten by the other creatures in the dockyard, even his own brothers and sisters. Eventually the duck mom loses faith and says, "I wish to goodness you were miles away."

Parental disapproval is painful but sometimes inevitable. You might not be able to *ever* convince your parents that what you're doing is important or worthwhile. But just understanding your parents' attitude toward your career can free you from that pervasive feeling of being a failure or being wrong. You might not be able to change their feelings, but you can separate them from your own self-image as an independent adult.

Family Influences
....

If you feel like an Ugly Duckling at work, examine the familial influences that might be a factor. Ask yourself these questions:

- What did my parents want me to be when I grew up?
- Which of their aspirations have I fulfilled? Which have I not fulfilled?
- Were their hopes for me influenced by gender stereotypes of their era?
- Are their attitudes limited by their own upbringing, education, social class, or experiences?
- How do they feel about my career now?
- Have I, or can I, accept that they might not always approve of my choices?

Even the most well-meaning parents can make a daughter feel like a duck out of water.

I was blessed with wonderful parents who were a great inspiration to me—and still are, although they have passed away. My father ran the family business and also took a great interest in our education and activities. My mother took care of five kids, yet still found time to do volunteer work. She wanted nothing but the best for all of us, but she was a woman of her times and it influenced her reactions.

I remember coming home from college brimming with excitement because I had finally figured out what I wanted to do with my career: go into the field of public relations. I expected a positive reception to my big news and was really shot down when my mother said, "Why don't you learn to be a medical records assistant instead?" She had heard about the daughter of a friend who was taking a course in this vocation and it sounded like a sensible, down-to-earth choice. My mother had suffered through financial instability in her youth and wanted me to have a stable, steady job (or better yet, a stable, bread-winning husband). Being in public relations sounded too glamorous, like shooting for the stars, and it put her off.

Women of my baby-boomer generation experienced a huge cultural shift between childhood and adulthood. Many of our parents expected us to grow up to be stay-at-home moms, and then the world turned upside down during the late 1960s and into the 1970s. Although many parents came to not only accept but admire our career choices and ambition, there is sometimes a lingering sense that we don't fit into the family mode.

Even if you're younger and didn't run into the generational divide about women's roles, there may be other reasons why you clash with your parents' expectations. Perhaps they expect too much of you because you've had opportunities that they did not. Or they'd like you to have a more secure career and not take risks. Or they wish you did something artistic while you prefer business. There are a million ways you can fail to fulfill your parents dreams—but that doesn't mean you're a failure. Sometimes you have to remind yourself that you're proud of your choices regardless of what other people think, even those who love you most.

Besides parents, you might be disheartened by other family members who don't recognize your potential or support your drive. A husband might worry—consciously or unconsciously—that his manhood is threatened if you earn more than he does. Children might fear that you won't be available to take care of them if you take on a new job or promotion. A female partner might suspect that you'll leave her behind if your career soars. Siblings and friends might feel that your drive and success only highlights their own shortcomings in comparison.

If your loved ones don't recognize you as a swan—or don't want you to be one—you need to show patience and understanding. Remember that their negativity may stem from insecurity—and even from love. They don't want to lose you. They don't want you to outgrow them or fly so high they can't follow. They don't want to seem like failures in comparison to you. It will take time to gain their support for your ambitions, but it is usually possible, if you continue to love them and to be yourself.

Sometimes, though, you may have to accept that your family and old friends are not going to be your greatest supporters. You have to look beyond them to find the people who believe you can soar.

Surround Yourself with Swans

Once the Ugly Duckling recognizes his own reflection as a swan, he is warmly accepted into the flock. "The big swans swam round and round him and stroked him with their bills. And the old swans bent their heads and did homage before him," the story goes. "The lilacs bent their boughs right into the water before him and the bright sun was warm and cheering."

While you're not likely to experience quite such a glorious reception in the corporate world, you can find a great deal of satisfaction when you surround yourself with people who recognize your strengths and appreciate your ideas. Some women are lucky enough to fall into a circle of supporters, but more often it takes a methodical effort to find and encourage them.

Cultivate Supporters in Your Own Company

The world of work is not inherently altruistic or supportive. People are not necessarily accepting, helpful, or even kind. But the office doesn't have to be a dog-eat-dog jungle. The truth is somewhere in between. People are busy and worried about their own survival. They have too much on their minds and desks to spend a whole lot of time thinking about their coworkers' needs and goals. It takes a proactive stance to cultivate support because it doesn't always happen spontaneously.

Help people. The number one way to turn people into supporters is to do them a favor—and not just once, but consistently.

Be forewarned that not everyone will respond the way you hope they will. Some coworkers will simply take advantage of your efforts to help them. Some people will take your favors, run with them, and never look back. Then you have a choice. You can either stop doing favors for that person, or the next time, figure out a way to ask a favor back (a big one) and see how the individual reacts. Typically, that person who has taken and run with your favors will be happy to respond by helping you in some way. He or she has just been too busy or self-absorbed to do something for you without being asked.

Deliver on what you say you will do. In a world full of empty promises, people really appreciate someone they can count on. If you say you'll have the research in an Excel spreadsheet by Monday, put it on the top of your list. If you promise to support someone else's idea in a meeting, be sure you speak up. If you say you'll give a coworker feedback on a draft of her report, do it on a timely basis so she can meet her deadline.

Praise a coworker. Give compliments to a colleague for something she's done—and mean it! Most people don't expect you to praise them, and when you do, they're surprised, almost shocked, and then they smile gratefully and you can see their shoulders relax. It's rewarding for the other person and for you—and it's free of charge.

Don't be a gossip. We're all human and sometimes indulge in a few snippets. But please try to avoid indulging in gossip. Although people may enjoy dishing with you at the moment, in the long run they'll think, "If she gossips about someone else, she'll gossip about me, too." If you want to avoid seeming too remote or frosty, you can indulge in a little harmless gossip about people you don't know, like celebrities or contestants on a reality TV show. But leave your coworkers out of the rumor mill.

Don't be a "yes-woman." Don't always be the one who agrees with or curries favor with the bosses. People can see through this and your staff may see you as the one who overloads them. This will *not* gain you supporters or leverage in the long run. There are some people who zoom up the ladder fast with this approach, but when the ride gets rocky they don't have a crew of supporters to help them out.

Look for connections—and something extra. Erin M. Fuller, executive director of the National Association of Women Business Owners (NAWBO), offered this advice about identifying who you want to cultivate within your organization. "We've all had the experience of observing someone and identifying some type of connection in how they express ideas, solve problems, their sense of humor. Look for someone who will probably experience some situations similarly to you, but will also give you perspective or institutional knowledge that will add more context to a new situation. To gain the perspective of someone who is in a different role or has a different skill-set is invaluable."

Deb Langford, who leads Time Warner's Worldwide Recruitment and Executive Search practice, shares this advice: "I always take networking and connecting to the next level. I rarely ask "what do you do?" Rather, I enjoy having an interesting conversation, and usually the dialogue includes their career passion, vision, and insights. Everyone should have several outstanding relationships within their organization and outside, with people from a multitude of backgrounds."

Find Supporters Outside of Your Organization

Joining an organization lets you find like-minded individuals who share your interests, passion, and drive. And an organization is a place to test your wings, so to speak. By heading up a committee and leading a group in a task or project, you are learning and exercising skills you may not have had the opportunity to use at work. Seeing your success and growing your support network builds confidence to take more risks and responsibilities at work.

Sharon Hadary, executive director of the Center for Women's Business Research, finds that the best way to become involved with supportive people outside of your company is by giving back.

"Join women's organizations and/or professional organizations and participate in programs," she suggests. "Share your knowledge and provide your support—and it will come back to you."

Join an industry group. Whatever your profession, you can bet there is a group to match it. You can research these by talking to other people at work or doing an online search. Joining an industry group is a commitment, so make sure you test the waters before you get involved. Look at the Web site and materials and, if possible, have coffee with someone who belongs to ask questions about the organization's goals, criteria for membership, and activities.

Find a crossover group. You don't have to limit yourself to a group that does exactly what you do or matches your profile perfectly. Open up your possibilities to crossover groups. I found invaluable support in NAWBO, even though I don't own a business. I identified with the women in this group and found they shared my work values and style. Check the "Resources" section of this book for some wonderful crossover support organizations for women.

Connect on the Internet. Networking and finding kindred spirits online is a growing trend. On one end of the spectrum are informal social networks that connect you to hundreds of friends and friends of friends. On the more serious business-minded side, there are Web sites that invite you to make connections and grow your professional network online. These sites are often used for referral-based job hunting, but they have other applications as well, such as finding potential business partners and reaching industry experts for advice and opinions. You have to be cautious when you contact people online, but the structure of some of the better Web sites lends them credibility.

Join a community, school, or religious group. Many women find a tremendous source of support in hobby clubs, Bible study circles, book clubs, and other groups unrelated to work. The support you find in these groups may or may not lead to networking opportunities, but regardless, it will enhance your overall sense of self-worth, and thereby give you more confidence on the job.

Create your own informal group. If you can't find an appealing group to join, consider creating one. Deirdre, a working mom, had a counterculture streak that made her resistant to established groups. Then she took her daughter to a small day care center with a progressive educational philosophy. This day care seemed to attract other parents who were a little outside the norm and Deirdre found common ground talking with them. Once the children had "graduated" and went on to different kindergartens, Deirdre found herself missing these women. So she organized once-a-month dinners for the day care moms— held at a casual Italian restaurant without kids, partners, or stress. The women found these dinners a great place to talk about their struggles to balance family and work with their evolving careers. From time to time, they offered each other tips about potential clients and job openings. But most importantly, they gave each other ongoing acceptance and encouragement.

Stay the Course as Support Ebbs and Flows

Finding and keeping supporters in the corporate world is a fluid endeavor. You can't rest on your laurels or count on a core group of supporters to stay enthusiastic, or even to be around. You can find your flock of swans—but sooner or later they will be flying in different directions. I've learned this lesson during the ten years since I started the Women On Their Way (WOTW) program.

During the first phrase of WOTW, the CEO loved it and was 100 percent behind me, but some in middle management were skeptical. I had to prove myself and show progress and results constantly. Nevertheless, I was so busy and overjoyed by the potential of the program that nothing slowed me down. I knew it was going to be successful and didn't want to miss a beat.

During the second phase, Women On Their Way began to be a proven success, demonstrating merit and revenue. I would show people letters and newspaper articles to prove how successful it was and that the sales numbers were rising. But some people would still roll their eyes and think it was ridiculous (although others thought it was great.) I kept trying to prove to *everyone* that the program was terrific, and frankly, this effort was exhausting. Even though I stayed the course, I gave the doubters too much energy.

Eventually I found the place where I am today. I've learned to ignore the criticism from those who don't matter in the big scheme of things, and listen to the criticism from those who do matter. I give the supporters as much attention and credence as the critics. Most importantly, I focus on letting others into the picture to share in the success of WOTW. I cultivate support not only by proving to people how terrifically well I am doing, but by opening up to their ideas and making sure they feel the program belongs to *everyone* on the team.

An interesting evolution occurred with this approach. I began to find supporters among men, especially young men, some fresh out of business school, a new breed entirely comfortable working on a woman's program. These bright young men are always coming into my office and giving me ideas, wanting to brainstorm.

However, sometimes the corporate world can be a lot like high school. The "teachers" (or more senior people like me) admire drive and enthusiasm and love it when you share ideas. But peers may try to hold you back, wanting you to be "cool," and not so ambitious. Your ambition can scare peers and make them feel less confident, so they mask their insecurity in derision.

Yet all companies need fresh ideas and youthful enthusiasm—from people at any age. So go ahead and engage the peers who share your vision and drive, and leave the rest behind. Talk to your immediate boss and even upper management about your ideas. Knock on doors, catch the CEO in the hallway…go for it!

And *never* let criticism break your spirit.

In fact, if you are not being criticized or ridiculed by someone in your organization then you're probably not stretching yourself enough. It is rare that people will sit around and say, "You know, Marcy is just doing such a great job, let's give her a lunch in her honor." More likely, if you're coming up with new ideas, you're rocking the boat rather than paddling along without making any waves. Some people are going to be impressed and excited, while others aren't going to like it. But it is your drive and original thinking that will propel the company and your career forward.

It may take time to get the recognition and support you deserve. You may have to wait for the right moment, when the corporate culture, the marketplace, and even society at large catch up with your ideas and aspirations. Be patient and remember that the recognition that is hard-won is often the most satisfying.

"He felt quite glad of all the misery and tribulation he had gone through, for he was the better able to appreciate his good fortune now and all the beauty which greeted him," wrote Hans Christian Andersen, about the Ugly Duckling's feelings upon being recognized as a swan.

Be persistent and keep moving right past those quacking ducks and naysaying hens. Just keep paddling toward your goals.

••

The Ugly Duckling on Wall Street

In the olden days but not so long ago, when most mommies stayed home to cook and clean while daddies brought home the bacon, a little girl named Olga was born, the youngest of three sisters.

When little Olga went to kindergarten she didn't want to play kitchen or babydoll like the other girls did. Instead, she liked to play with blocks and do puzzles by herself. By second grade she wanted to play checkers or flashcards after school, instead of dress-up with her sisters. And in junior high, when all the girls started sneaking on frosted lipstick and talking about boys for hours on their princess phones, Olga discovered a different passion: the world of high finance. While the other girls studied fashion magazines, she scrutinized the stock tables. And so some of the kids at school called her the Ugly Duckling.

When senior year of high school approached, Olga told her parents she wanted to go to a prestigious business school that was far afield.

"But Olga, why can't you go to the community college like your sisters did?" asked her mother. "After all, girls really just go to college to find someone to marry. Why go so far?"

"But I don't want to get married and have babies," said Olga. "I want a career in finance!"

"Not get married? Oh Olga, I don't know what to do with you," sighed her mother. "You might as well go away to college, then."

So Olga went far away to study business, hoping to find other birds of a feather. But there were hardly any young women in her class, and they were all working too hard to have time for friends. And on weekends the young men invited dates from the local girls' college to their fraternity parties, since they thought the few female classmates in their business school were odd ducks. Poor Olga swallowed her loneliness and threw herself into her studies.

When she graduated, she went to work in a financial services firm. Some of the men thought she was a secretary and asked her to bring coffee, but when they found out that she was on the investment side, they shunned her. She wasn't invited to their club lunches or weekend golf games. Olga's hard work won her the grudging respect of some of her colleagues, but she still felt like the Ugly Duckling.

As Olga ate lonely lunches at her desk and looked out the window at the bustling city, she knew that there had to be other women out there who shared her ambitions. Since she couldn't do a quick Internet search in those days, she let her fingers do the walking, and found a group in the phone book called Women Flying High In Finance.

Olga went to a conference the group was holding at a nearby hotel with a large fountain in the atrium. She sat quietly in the back of the meeting room, impressed by the poised, savvy women. "These *women are so smart and confident," she thought, "They'll never want to talk to someone like me." So she glided out of the conference and went back to her office.*

After another cold, bleak winter in the windy caverns of Wall Street, spring bloomed, and with it, hope. Olga decided to take her brown bag lunch outside to eat at a fountain in a nearby plaza, where the sound and spray of the water was soothing. There she watched as dozens and dozens of working women zipped by. And she had an idea. All these women had paychecks. They needed advice on how to save, protect, and invest their money. What about an investment program geared toward women?

Filled with hope, Olga took her idea to her boss at the firm. But he scoffed at her idea and blew smoke rings in her direction. "Most women don't have enough money to invest, and even if they do, they don't have a head for investing," he said.

Yet Olga saw the big picture and knew there must be a place for her idea! If you "pooled" the money from thousands of women who did have control over their money, there was quite a big market of new customers who were untapped.

Remembering the splendid group of Women Flying High In Finance, she called up the chairwoman and asked for a meeting. The chair brought along three other members, who all thought Olga's idea was brilliant. With their connections, Olga was able to find a financial services firm that wanted to launch her program. She left her old job behind and went to work at the new company, where, after much hard work, Olga found supporters among her clients, her coworkers, and eventually the board.

Now, when she went to work, she basked in the bright warmth of people who shared her vision and work values. She had never dared to hope for such happiness.

But Olga was not content to rest in her feathered nest. She was busy planning how she would bring her women's investment program to the next level by the following spring.

Fairy Dust from *The Ugly Duckling*

- Recognize your own strengths and talents even if you're not yet appreciated at work.
- Give yourself a pat on the back instead of waiting for other people to praise you.
- Accept that not everyone will be a supporter and don't let it diminish your sense of selfworth.
- Cultivate supporters in your company by doing other people favors, delivering on what you promise, and giving co-workers deserved praise.
- Surround yourself with other "swans" by joining an industry group or a crossover group.
- Look for like-minded supportive people by joining or forming groups outside the work realm.
- Further your skills and education in an area that you've always aspired to with others you've always wanted to get to know in those fields.
- Stay the course as support ebbs and flows, and keep paddling toward your goal!

CHAPTER 6

···

Thumbelina

Think Big, Show Initiative, and Do Well by Doing Good

THUMBELINA MAY BE THE SMALLEST FAIRY TALE HEROINE, BUT SHE IS also the pluckiest. This tiny dynamo doesn't always ask permission or do whatever the higher-ups tell her to do. She does what she knows is right and speaks her mind. She understands the limits of loyalty. And she is not afraid to take risks to find her place in the sun.

This beloved Hans Christian Andersen story, originally called "Little Tiny," is a charming parable of a diminutive girl with big dreams and lofty ideals. It speaks to people of all ages who feel small and inconsequential, yet determined to stand up for their right to freedom and fulfillment.

Here is the synopsis of the story of this miniature role model.

A woman who cannot have a child asks a fairy for help. The fairy gives her a barleycorn, which grows into a beautiful tulip. Within the flower there is a graceful little maiden no bigger than a thumb. She lives happily with the woman, sleeping in a walnut shell and floating on a tulip petal, singing sweetly. But her singing attracts the attention of a mean old toad, who wants Thumbelina to marry her son.

The toad steals Thumbelina away while she is sleeping and strands her on a leaf in the middle of a marsh. She escapes with the help of some fish and a butterfly, finally landing in a forest. There, she makes a home for herself, but when winter comes she cannot survive alone.

Thumbelina finds shelter in the house of a field mouse, in exchange for cleaning and storytelling services. A rich mole comes to visit the field mouse, and although blind, he falls in love with Thumbelina because of her enchanting songs and stories. The mole brings her into a passageway where they find a swallow who appears to be dead. The mouse and the mole consider the bird worthless, but Thumbelina sneaks back to care for him. When she finds that the swallow is not dead, just numb with cold, she nurses him back to health. After the swallow recovers, he asks Thumbelina to sit on his back and fly away with him. But Thumbelina is still loyal to the mouse and says she cannot go.

Then Thumbelina finds out that the greedy mouse, impressed by the mole's wealth, is planning to marry her off to him against her will. But just before the wedding, the swallow returns. This time Thumbelina hops on his back gladly and flies away. The bird lands her on a white flower at the bottom of a marble palace. Inside the flower, Thumbelina finds a beautiful little man who is the king of all the tiny creatures who dwell in the flowers. They marry, and as a wedding gift Thumbelina gets a tiny pair of wings, so she can finally fly on her own.

Think Big and Take the Initiative

Thumbelina is only half the length of a thumb, or about one inch tall, yet she thinks big. She never lets her lack of stature limit her hopes for the future or her willingness to take the initiative.

When you work for a big organization, you can feel like a tiny cog in the machine, insignificant in the vast scope of the corporate structure. To counteract this oppressive feeling, it's crucial to make a conscious effort to think bigger.

Melinda Bush is president and CEO of HRW Holdings LLC/ Hospitality Resources Worldwide. She is also about six feet tall with long blonde hair—more a spitting image of Rapunzel than Thumbelina, in fact. But like the little fairy tale character, Melinda believes in thinking big. She gives the advice to "Be bold" and tape a note card to your bathroom mirror with this slogan so you can read it every morning when you first wake up. She also suggests keeping a "platinum Rolodex" for both vertical (upwardly mobile) and horizontal (peer) contacts, filling your life with diverse channels and networks of people.

Five Steps to Increase Your Stature

1. Recognize that you bring a unique set of skills and talents to the company.
2. Notice how crucial your contribution is to the team.
3. Ask for a chance to take on more responsibility or lead a project.
4. Introduce an original idea for a product or service. And keep doing this.
5. Learn a new skill, and use it at work to further a company goal or a boss's project.
6. Exercise an entrepreneurial spirit within the framework of your organization.

The Entrepreneurial Drive

We're all familiar with the legendary success of women entrepreneurs who started their own companies: Oprah, Lillian Vernon, Esteé Lauder, Eileen Fisher, Kate Spade, and many others. These women differ in product, philosophy, and clientele, but they all share certain characteristics of successful entrepreneurs:

- Great passion for their work and their products
- Profound belief they will succeed
- Respect for and identification with their clients
- The drive to keep going through obstacles and setbacks

An entrepreneur is defined as "a risk-taking businessperson; someone who sets up and finances new commercial enterprises to make a profit." Yet entrepreneurs are inspired by more than the desire for wealth. Their primary motivation, in fact, is the need to realize their vision and goals. To turn their vision into reality, entrepreneurs need confidence, the charisma to excite and inspire other people, and a strong tolerance for risk-taking.

Many women dream of starting their own businesses, and many take the plunge. According to the Center for Women's Business Research, between 1997 and 2004 the growth in the number of 50-percent-or-more women-owned firms was nearly twice the rate of all firms. In 2004 there were 10.6 million privately-held, 50-percent-or-more women-owned firms, generating $2.46 trillion in sales and employing 19.1 million people worldwide.

Yet despite these impressive statistics, there is a downside to the explosion of entrepreneurship. According to the United States Small Business Administration, half of small businesses fail within the first year. Although figures differ on the longer-term rate of survival, the consensus is that about 80 percent of new businesses fail within the first five years.

You might not be able or inclined to take on the financial risk of starting a business. Perhaps you prefer the stability of a salaried job. Or you see the benefits of working with the financial and human resources of a large organization instead of going it alone. I started my own business when I was 29, but then sold it and eventually went back to corporate life. And I have found a tremendous opportunity to think and act as an entrepreneur within the corporate structure.

Keeping your day job does not necessarily mean you have to stifle your inclination to be an entrepreneur. Instead, with the cushion of a company behind you, you can excel by exhibiting these key entrepreneurial qualities.

Take appropriate risks. If someone asks if you want to give a presentation, say "yes" even though the thought of speaking in front of people makes your knees buckle. If there's a chance to get training in a new system that no one else in the company knows how to use, sign up. If there's a position opening up that's a stretch in terms of responsibility and skills, apply for it. You'll grow into the challenge. Don't settle for the role of the mole!

Take on more than your job description requires. If you want a bigger job, expand the one you already have. Look for ways you can do more than what is required. Come up with ideas to increase sales. Figure out how to streamline a sluggish procedure. Volunteer for a committee or ask to be included in more meetings. Learn a new technical skill or brush up on your speaking skills. You'll find that most bosses don't mind if you do *more* than expected, only less. And when you voluntarily take on more they start looking at you as someone who has potential for a bigger position and better pay.

I would love to spend more evenings curling up on the sofa with my husband, watching classic movies and munching popcorn. But instead I can usually be found in an airport lobby waiting for a flight to a speaking engagement, or sitting at my desk working late on a project that is above and beyond my job description. I'm not required to do half of what I do, but my inner drive sets the pace—a fast one!

No one ever made it to the top—or even halfway up—by just doing what she was told to do. Women, even more than men, have to prove themselves by constantly looking for means to increase their value to the company, enhance their stature and reputation in the industry, and go beyond the basics in every way they can.

Raise your own bar. Entrepreneurs are always setting higher and higher goals for themselves. But when people work for salaries and don't have that direct profit incentive, they may get lackadaisical.

If you want to climb the corporate ladder of success, it is essential to constantly raise your own bar. Otherwise you'll stay where the organizational seating chart has you pigeon-holed.

If you're already meeting your sales quota, strive to be in the top five percent of salespeople instead. If your boss is satisfied with your work, find out what you can do next year that would serve the team even better. If a system is working effectively but could be better, research how to improve it.

Don't drift along without any direction. Don't be complacent. Raise your expectations—and then exceed them.

Georgette "Gigi" Dixon, senior vice president and manager of national relationships for Wachovia, has this advice for women who want to be entrepreneurial within the corporate setting. "Become a thought leader and champion for change. Position yourself as a catalyst, someone who thrives on challenging the status quo while finding ways to gain a competitive advantage or differentiate your institution among its peers."

Prove you are passionate about your work. Entrepreneurs are intensely passionate about their ideas, their products, and their services. They *must* be passionate, or they would never be able to attract investors and customers!

In the salaried world, too, passion is what separates people who succeed from those who plateau or stagnate in their careers.

"Passion, purpose, and perseverance have been the words I have lived by in my career," says Dee Rogers, director of base operations for Northwest Airlines. "Passion for the job you're doing makes people realize you're the best at what you do. Purpose enables you to understand what you want and what it will take to get there. Finally, there's perseverance. Everything that I have gotten has been made better by the fact that I stuck with it until I was sure that I had done everything I could."

Pay attention to details and small steps. Successful entrepreneurs have the ability to zero in on details and focus on incremental steps that contribute to their larger vision. They will spend a limitless amount of time reworking a design, wooing a new client, addressing the tiniest kinks in a system—whatever it takes.

"It's all about small steps," says Gail Evans, bestselling author and former executive vice president of the CNN Newsgroup. "People say, 'I want to save my knowledge or power for the big issues.' But business is about the small issues."

Remember the basics. My aunt, Harriette M. Beeson, owned a bookstore in Memphis for 16 years. As one of the only women business owners I knew well, she was a role model for me growing up. Looking back on her time as a small business owner, Harriette says, "The things I learned in my 16 years were to face up to decisions, return phone calls right away, work on keeping good relations with publishers and wholesalers, and pay bills on time." Certainly these rules are good basics to follow for anyone working with an entrepreneurial spirit inside or outside a corporation!

Intrapreneurs

In 1985 the author and consultant Gifford Pinchot wrote a landmark book called *Intrapreneuring: Why You Don't Have to Leave the Corporation to Become an Entrepreneur.* His thesis was that corporations must innovate to survive, and therefore should encourage creative people to become entrepreneurs within the company structure by giving them the freedom and resources they need to pursue their visions.

This concept took off to such an extent that the word now merits an entry in the *American Heritage Dictionary:* "Intrapreneur: a person within a large corporation who takes direct responsibility for turning an idea into a profitable finished product through assertive risk-taking and innovation."

Intrapreneurs and entrepreneurs share many characteristics. They have original ideas in which they strongly believe. They are motivated by a desire to see their vision through to fruition, not merely to get rich (although that is always a welcome by-product). They are capable of intense dedication, focus, and hard work. And they thrive when they can forge ahead and take action, without waiting for permission and process.

Know How High You Can Fly

Many women are compelled to start their own businesses because they chafe under restrictions and boundaries. And when you work in a corporate structure, there *are* certain limitations. You have to discern how to balance your entrepreneurial drive with sensitivity to your company's parameters and politics. Women who thrive as intrapreneurs are adept at the art of being independent without overstepping boundaries.

"Spend time building relationships with high-level executives, establishing your credibility and integrity among them," suggests Gigi Dixon. "Tell them what you would like to accomplish for the business. Validate your vision for business success with the mission and values of the company. If you desire to build influence, know what does or can make your organization a leader among its peer institutions."

How to Get Your Own Wings in a Corporation

- Try to gain your immediate boss's support for your idea or project first.
- Generate enthusiasm for your idea among your coworkers and include them on the team.

(continued)

- Be well prepared when you present your concept or project to the higher-ups. Back up your ideas with research.
- Be sensitive to timing. A boss might love your bold idea when she's fresh and rested at 10 A.M., but may have a negative reaction if you introduce it during her afternoon slump.
- If your boss is not enthusiastic and you want to go over her head to a higher-up, analyze the company politics first.
- Err on the side of caution when you project timelines and results. It won't hurt if the project goes quicker or better than you forecast, but the inverse will damage your credibility.
- Once you achieve results, appropriately publicize them through e-mails, reports, presentations, company newsletters, industry organizations, and even the media, if necessary.

It seems incredible now, but when I first brought up the idea of a program for women business travelers, many people thought this market was too small and inconsequential a clientele to pursue. But my boss at the time was swept up in my enthusiasm and said "go for it." Then she left the company, and it was over a year before she was replaced. During this time, I continued to mold the program and attract more and more women to stay at the new Wyndham hotels that were popping up monthly around the country. It was an exhilarating period, working without a boss, not asking permission, creating results. I was doing what I knew was right and good for the company, and basking in my independence.

Then, however, a new boss came in and someone told him that I was not a team player. Here I was building clientele and driving revenue, but someone didn't like that I was so independent, so a seed of doubt was planted in my new boss's mind. Well, my immediate reaction was to be defensive and badmouth the naysayer, but I decided to take the high road. And before too long, my new boss could see how valuable I was to the company and became a wholehearted supporter of the Women On Their Way program. The boss also realized that while I am a team player, I need a certain amount of autonomy to flourish. And so I've been able to follow my passion in a company that allows me to work independently.

Over the years I've learned to ride out difficult periods and keep my attention focused on my goals. I also strive to treat all my coworkers with respect and fairness, through boom times and slumps (although believe me, I'm not perfect at this). But I simply refuse to buy into the idea that you have to be greedy, selfish, or mean to succeed in business. In the long run, I believe that the opposite holds true. Positive actions will usually reap good results, sooner or later. And meanwhile, you'll be able to go to sleep with a clear conscience.

Do What You Know Is Right

Thumbelina does not rescue the helpless swallow because she expects anything in return. She takes care of the bird because her heart leads her to do the right thing. And her altruistic act brings her an unexpected benefit.

Of course, in the business world you can't expect all your good actions to be reciprocated in kind. There may be times when you're betrayed or at least unappreciated by the very people you help. But by and large, you will gain distinct advantages by treating people with decency and consideration. You'll be able to hold your head up even if you are maligned or double-crossed. You'll inspire the support of the majority of your coworkers and the respect of peers in other companies. And you may find that someone you treat well proves to be an unexpected but important ally, like the swallow in the Thumbelina story.

During a major reorganization, Maggie's company was downsizing many employees. One of Maggie's colleagues, Sarah, was on the list of those being let go. Suddenly people who had formerly been friendly with Sarah avoided her like the plague, as if getting laid off was contagious.

Although Maggie had never been close to Sarah, she figured she could use a friendly chat. Trying to keep the conversation light, Maggie told Sarah about a book she had just finished that was fun and uplifting, a good bedside read. Sarah asked if she could borrow the book, and Maggie said sure, and brought it in the next day, which was Sarah's last at the company. A week later, Sarah e-mailed Maggie to tell her that the book had been a saving grace and welcome diversion from what was happening.

About a year later Maggie heard that Sarah had landed a terrific job with a Fortune 500 company. By this time, Maggie herself had been laid off and was looking for a new position. She contacted Sarah, who was glad to help Maggie get an interview. Maggie was hired, and on her first day at the new job, she found the long-ago borrowed book on her desk, with a note from Sarah saying, "Glad I had a chance to return this!"

In the media, there's a tendency to emphasize the ruthless side of business. And while it may be scintillating to look at the corporate world as a gladiator ring, the reality is another story. True, the business world can be cruel, unfair, uncaring, and dysfunctional. But I believe that it doesn't have to go in this direction. As more and more women assume positions of power, we're learning that we can flourish by cooperating and boosting each other up, instead of putting each other down.

There is no instant karma or heavenly reward here in the corporate world. Initiative can be seen as lack of teamwork, integrity met with deceit, fairness repaid with backstabbing. But these factors generally level out if you stay the course and continue to do what you know is right. People who treat others like dirt sometimes make a fast ascent, but they usually crash before too long. I've seen time and again that the women with career longevity are those who act with integrity and treat other people with consideration.

You *can* be a player in the business world and still follow the Golden Rule: *Do unto others as you would have them do unto you.*

Many top women executives embrace the idea of creating a win-win atmosphere within the corporation. They know that treating people well is not only the right moral choice, it is also the best strategy for ensuring a dedicated, loyal, and ambitious staff that drives the company to success.

Wendy Lopez is CEO of the Lopez Garcia group, a large engineering firm that employs about 300 people. "I believe in giving people opportunities, then providing them with support and encouragement," she says. "If they are successful, then the company is successful. You must create an atmosphere where people know they are appreciated and supported in order to get the best they can give. Set the course and give them the opportunity and responsibility to achieve greatness."

Michelle Peluso, CEO of Travelocity, inspires loyalty with a number of innovative methods. "We give out awards each week in my e-mail for employees demonstrating innovation or urgency or passion. Employees are nominated by their peers for great work, and I award one or two people each week in my e-mail, where I call out their accomplishments and the winner gets a small cash bonus," she says. "We celebrate successes and even sometimes what we learn from failures. I expect a lot from my team but they also know I'll be there with them during the hard times. I have brown bag lunches two times a week with employees of all levels to find out what's on their mind, obstacles in their way, et cetera."

The Limits of Loyalty

When the swallow recovers the use of his wing and is ready to escape from the mole's lair, he invites Thumbelina to come along. Although she longs to fly out into the warm sunshine, she stays out of loyalty to the field mouse who gave her refuge in winter. Soon after, however, the field mouse announces that Thumbelina is to be married to the despicable mole and must spend her life underground without seeing the sunshine or flowers ever again. When Thumbelina refuses, the avaricious mouse tries to bully her into submission with a nasty threat: "Now don't be obstinate or I shall bite you with my teeth."

This aspect of the fairy tale brings up interesting questions about the limits of loyalty. We've all heard the story of the people who were laid off after years of service with no gold watch or golden parachute. People used to think that loyalty would be repaid with job security and retirement benefits—but now these expectations seem naïve. The concept of loyalty to the company has undergone a sea change in the last ten to twenty years.

Still, while most people no longer believe that their company will reward loyalty by taking care of them, loyalty persists for other reasons. Unemployment is a major worry and many people are rightly concerned about holding on to the jobs they already have. Or they are loyal to the company because they like the people, the boss, the location, the salary, or the work itself.

Women sometimes exhibit greater loyalty to their companies then men. We want to believe that we will be treasured for our hard work when, in fact, hard work is expected and doesn't win us any guarantees.

You have to face the cold, hard fact that you can't expect loyalty from the company unless you continue to contribute and show results. In the film business they say, "You're only as good as your last picture." In the corporation it translates to "You're only as good as your last quarterly report."

Women are inclined to take it personally when a boss gives them a critical performance review, or fails to recommend them for a raise or promotion. But in the modern American workplace, loyalty is based on mutual advantage. Loyalty can only be expected if you make your boss look good and prove yourself with consistent results.

Don't expect loyalty just because you think your boss is fond of you or knows that you're trying hard. You can expect that type of loyalty from your family, old friends, and canine companions. But when it comes to workplace, it's all business, and if you don't come up with the goods, loyalty will evaporate.

With this reality in mind, you may decide to redefine your own concept of loyalty in the workplace. Loyalty to a certain boss or the company as a whole is no longer a given; it is a choice. And the choices can be confusing. You have to analyze what constitutes merited and appropriate loyalty—and know when to draw the line.

Loyalty Litmus Test

Answer these questions "yes" or "no."

- Do I believe in the company mission and fit into the company culture?
- Do I truly enjoy the day-to-day work?
- Do I get good raises?
- Do I have good benefits?
- Does my boss treat me with respect and show appreciation?
- Do I enjoy working with my peers and feel valued as a team member?
- Does my company give me opportunities to develop my education and skills?
- Is there room for promotion?
- Does this job allow me to juggle work and family (through flexible hours, telecommuting, generous time off, etc.)

If you answer "yes" to most of these questions, you have good reason to be loyal. If you answer "no" to a majority of questions, this company does not deserve your unconditional loyalty. Expand your network and keep your eyes open for an opportunity to move on.

Where you place your loyalty is also linked to individual values. Many women deeply value appreciation, praise, and recognition. A boss who says "You did a great job" or an Employee of the Week award can fuel some people's loyalty. For others, financial compensation is the primary criterion for loyalty and they ascribe to the belief that the paycheck is the thanks. Some people value the chance to be creative on the job, or have a boss and colleagues who are fun. You have to weigh your values when deciding who or what merits your loyalty.

When to Draw the Line

Sometimes bosses or companies try to seduce employees into doing something dishonest or unethical by playing the loyalty card. This is a blatant abuse of loyalty and should never be tolerated. Make no mistake about it. Anyone who asks you to do something that compromises your values or your honesty does not deserve your loyalty.

Don't buy into the myth that playing along will gain you their loyalty either. Beware of "corporate amnesia." If your boss asks you to do something unethical and you do it, he or she will inevitably deny they gave the order if you are found out.

If your boss asks you to do something unethical or dishonest, consider these responses:

- Your boss may not realize that the request is unethical, so explain why you think it is. He or she may need a wake-up call.
- If you have an easygoing relationship with your boss, humor or incredulity can sometimes diffuse the situation. Try saying: "You want me to do *what?* Oh, you must be kidding…I must have heard you wrong…that can't possibly be what you mean."
- Conveniently forget to do the objectionable assignment or put it on the back burner and don't get to it (however, don't apply this passive-aggressive tactic to your regular work).

Your boss might be reluctant to press the issue if she knows she's asking you to do something wrong.

- Your boss could be deflecting something that his boss told him to do, and looking for someone else to do a dirty job, so tread carefully if you think of going to a higher-up.
- Ask your boss to document the request in writing. Respond in writing why you object.
- If you're in a public company, point to or reference the Sarbanes-Oxley Law of 2002, which holds public companies to tight standards.
- If your boss still insists that you do something objectionable, you may have to go to human resources and/or the legal department. If possible, ask someone you trust in one of these departments how to proceed first. If you have a mentor inside or outside the company, ask for guidance.

Dumb but Not Dishonest

If your boss wants you to do something that you believe is not a smart move for the company, but it's not unethical, it places a different demand on your sense of loyalty. Consider this sequence of responses:

1. Ask questions and be open-minded if your boss is willing to explain her decision. She may have more knowledge of why you or the company should go forward with an action that seems ill-advised.
2. Bring up reasons why you disagree. Write down your viewpoint and send it via e-mail so you create a record. If your recommendations are ignored, as least you voiced your opinion.
3. If you think it's the stupidest idea in the world and will sink the company, discuss it with someone else in the company you trust—a mentor if possible, or a peer or a more senior higher-up boss.

Hopefully, one of these scenarios will stop the misguided course of action in its tracks. But in the end, if your boss insists that you do something that you think is a bad move, but not dishonest one, you may have to go ahead and do it. If this happens often, however, you should consider transferring your loyalty elsewhere.

The Loyalty of Letting Go

The swallow loves Thumbelina and wishes he could keep her with him in his lofty nest atop a marble palace. But he knows she would be more comfortable living in a beautiful white flower on terra firma. "You must choose for yourself one of those lovely flowers and I will put you down on it," the swallow says. "And then you shall have everything you can wish to make you happy."

Sometimes we have to let go of what we love at work. Or a mentor has to let a mentee go. You might launch a product or project and then see the wisdom of handing the reins to people who can do more to advance it. Your boss might be great, but if there's no room for promotion in his or her department you need to move on. If you're ambitious, you might have to leave a company where you're comfortable to pursue bigger opportunities elsewhere.

At Thumbelina's wedding, "the best gift was a pair of beautiful wings which had belonged to a large white fly. And they fastened them to her shoulders so that she might fly from flower to flower." True happiness comes to the little heroine when she can finally fly on her own, no longer dependent on a butterfly or a bird to soar. How proud the swallow was! And a good mentor will be proud, too, when your career takes off.

Ultimately, your loyalty has to belong to your own career goals and potential. There is no inherent disloyalty in leaving to find greater job satisfaction. In fact, bosses and coworkers who are truly loyal to you will accept that you have to move—or even help you fly off.

....

Tina Thumbelina

Once upon a time there was a young woman named Tina who was so petite that her friends and family called her Tina Thumbelina. When she went to work for a large telecommunications firm, however, she was careful not to let anyone hear the nickname because she knew it diminished her credibility. And it was already hard enough to be taken seriously when she was so small that you could easily miss her in a room. Fortunately, she had three older brothers, and so she had learned to be assertive.

Tina had to work twice as hard as men in the office to prove herself and get promoted. Finally, after five years of dedicated work for the company, she attained a managerial position with a supportive, congenial team. She even had her own little office on the fourteenth floor, with tall windows to let in the morning light and nourish the flowering potted plants she enjoyed growing.

But one day Tina was informed by management that they were moving her to another division, where the supervisor had a dreadful reputation. "I won't go work for that toad," Tina told her friends. "I'll get another job instead."

Tina left her company and started her job search with a great sense of adventure and optimism. But after six months of searching without any nibbles, she felt small and lost, floating without any direction.

Finally she found a job at a mega-corporation, where she was assigned to a windowless cubicle. The position was a step down, but someplace to survive until the industry picked up. "There are so many people looking for work I could have hired someone with more experience," her new boss told Tina. "But I felt sorry for you."

The new boss looked as mousy as a librarian, but was crafty as a fox when it came to company politics. One day she said to Tina, "If I were you, I wouldn't have lunch with Sally anymore. She's on her way out." Tina was surprised to hear this news about her coworker, since Sally was bright and diligent. "I'm just warning you, that relationship is not worth saving," said the boss.

Tina continued to have lunch with Sally anyway, and discreetly gave her a heads-up about the office rumors. Thanks to Tina, Sally was able to find a better job before she was laid off. Sally suggested that Tina also apply at her new company, but Tina said no. "My boss hired me above more experienced people. I feel like I owe it to her to stay now that I'm up to speed."

Tina kept plugging away in the dull fluorescent light of her cubicle. Then one gloomy Monday her boss asked her to "adjust" the figures their department was submitting for the quarterly report. "I don't think that's the right thing to do," Tina replied. "You must be making a mistake."

The boss turned nasty. "The word is coming down from higher up than me," she said. "And you'd better do what they say or you'll be in the bull's-eye!"

Now Tina realized that she had made a terrible mistake in not following Sally to the other company. When she called Sally to talk about the situation, her friend said, "As much as I'd love to work with you, I think you'd do better at a smaller firm where you'll be noticed more. Let me put you in contact with a couple of people who might help."

Tina followed up with the leads, and sent Sally a vase of white tulips as a thank-you gift when one of them resulted in a job offer. And that was how Tina landed a job at a small but growing telecommunications company, where she had a sunny little office of her own.

....

Fairy Dust from *Thumbelina*

- Think big no matter what your professional stature.
- Exercise an entrepreneurial spirit within your company. Take risks, show initiative, and raise your own bar.
- Balance your entrepreneurial drive with sensitivity to your organization's parameters and politics.

- Treat coworkers on all levels with respect and kindness, and you can do well by doing good.
- Realize that you can't expect loyalty from the company unless you continue to contribute and show results.
- Anyone who asks you to do something dishonest or unethical does not deserve your loyalty.
- Sometimes you have to let go of a boss or company you love to seek bigger opportunities elsewhere.

CHAPTER 7

....

Sleeping Beauty

Be Inclusive and Wake Up to Your Full Potential

SLEEPING BEAUTY'S FATHER, THE KING, MAKES A DECISION WITH disastrous consequences when he excludes one fairy from the christening feast of his daughter. This mistake sets off a chain of events that nearly dooms his entire court, as well as his beloved daughter. In the workplace, too, exclusion can lead to big trouble: discrimination, poor employee morale, and even that modern-day version of the fairy's curse—costly litigation.

It is ironic that a lesson about inclusion can be found in *Sleeping Beauty*, which strikes many people as the fairy tale that is most antithetical to progressive thinking. Sleeping Beauty herself (also called the princess, Briar Rose, or Aurora), is among the most passive of fairy tale heroines. She doesn't work; she doesn't seek adventure, and her only significant action—touching the spindle—is preordained by the fairy's curse. She is immediately punished for her brief flirtation with independence, only to be rescued by the Prince. It's enough to cause nightmares in any liberated mom reading a bedtime story!

Despite her limitations, *Sleeping Beauty* has a long and illustrious history. Early echoes of the story are found in *Perceforest*, an Arthurian romance first printed in 1528, and in Giambattista

Basile's tale "Sun, Moon, and Thalia" of 1636. Charles Perrault included *Sleeping Beauty* as the first story in his famous 1697 collection. These early versions do not end with Sleeping Beauty and the prince living happily ever after. They go on to tell what happens after the marriage, and it isn't pretty. It turns out that the prince's mother is an ogress who tries to boil and eat their two children and the princess! Fortunately, by this time Sleeping Beauty has grown more assertive, and she flips the plot so that the ogress ends up in a vat of boiling serpents and toads.

This disturbing and incongruous plot line was dropped by the Grimm Brothers when they published the tale as "Briar Rose." The Grimm version ends the way most of us remember the story: with an awakening kiss and a wedding. Here is a synopsis of the simpler tale.

A king and a queen plan a lavish christening feast for their baby girl. The king has only twelve golden plates, so the thirteenth fairy in the kingdom is not invited. At the feast, eleven of the fairies bestow favorable gifts upon the baby: virtue, modesty, wit, beauty, riches, and so on. But when the thirteenth fairy appears, she is angry at being spurned and proclaims a curse: "The princess shall prick herself with a spindle in her fifteenth year and fall down dead." However the twelfth fairy softens the blow by saying, "It shall not be death, but a deep sleep lasting a hundred years into which your daughter shall fall."

The king proclaims that all the spindles in the land must be destroyed. But on her fifteenth birthday the princess wanders up to the attic of the castle and finds an old lady spinning. The girl pricks herself on the spindle and the curse is fulfilled: she falls asleep, as does everyone and everything in the entire castle.

A dense hedge of briar roses grows around the castle. Many gallant princes try to penetrate the hedge, but they are always caught by the thorns and perish. Then, just as the hundred years of the curse ends, a prince arrives. The briar hedge parts for him and he enters the castle unharmed. He kisses Sleeping Beauty and her eyes open. The whole court awakes, and the couple has a splendid wedding.

Sleeping Beauty captured the Romantic imagination and inspired one of the great classic ballets, choreographed by Marius Petipa, with music by Peter Ilyich Tchaikovsky. The ballet premiered in St. Petersburg in 1890, and has been performed by major companies around the world every since. George Balanchine, the premier choreographer of the twentieth century, made his childhood debut as Cupid in this ballet, and Rudolph Nureyev made his sensational debut in the West dancing the role of the prince.

The Tchaikovsky score was also used in *Sleeping Beauty*'s next incarnation: the Walt Disney animated feature of 1959. This film is one of Disney's most artistic works, with beautifully detailed hand-drawn backgrounds and enchanting songs like "Once Upon a Dream" sung by a lilting soprano. Sleeping Beauty, or Aurora, as she is called in the Disney film, became a superstar of Disney World. Now, as a member of the Disney Princesses group, her flowing blonde hair adorns a never-ending array of merchandise.

Unlike *Cinderella*, however, *Sleeping Beauty* never inspired a rash of girl-power movies that update her story. Instead, her passivity has provoked a storm of politically correct criticism and is often cited as an example of the harmful female stereotypes that fairy tales perpetuate.

Without disputing that Sleeping Beauty is not the greatest role model for modern girls, let's give her a break and focus on the valuable contemporary lesson within the tale: the danger of exclusion and the need to be thoughtfully inclusive in order for the individual and the whole company to flourish.

Claim Your Place at the Table

In the Perrault version of *Sleeping Beauty*, the king has special table settings made for seven of the eight fairies in the kingdom, who are served on "a magnificent cover with a case of massive gold, wherein were a spoon, knife, and fork, all of pure gold set with diamonds and rubies." When the eighth fairy shows up, the king "could not furnish her with a case of gold because he had only seven made," since he didn't think the eighth fairy was worth inviting.

Women in the workforce can feel like the fairy who is not invited to the feast and, when she shows up anyway, doesn't get the first-rate place setting.

When I showed up at the U.S. Capitol building in 1982 to start my new job as assistant press secretary to Senate Majority Leader Howard Baker, I was gung-ho and ready for work. I was, after all, *the* assistant press secretary. Well, I had shown up, but my title also meant I had to start at the bottom and work my way up, and that meant lots of grunt work!

The Glass Ceiling in the Banquet Hall

Women certainly are showing up to partake of the feast in droves. According to the U.S. Department of Labor, in 2003 women comprised 47 percent of the total labor force. Over 68.2 million women were in the civilian labor force, 64.4 million of whom were employed in 2003.

Yes, women are showing up. But are they getting their fair share of those golden plates and jeweled utensils? According to a 2004 report from the Institute for Women's Policy Research, females earned 76 cents for every dollar males earned (up from 73 cents in 2002).

And when it comes to promotion to the highest corporate positions, the glass ceiling still exists, although it is showing cracks. In 2004, only eight Fortune 500 companies were run by women, and a total of 16 Fortune 1000 companies had women in the top spot. According to Catalyst, in 2002 only 15.7 percent of corporate officers were women.

Still, these figures do reflect some progress. Since 1995, the number of women in the highest officer positions in corporate America has increased 113 percent. Since the year 2000, there has been a 5.2 percent increase in the number of women corporate officers in Fortune 500 companies. We're getting there, but we're not there yet.

"I do believe there is still a glass ceiling," says Sharon Hadary, executive director of the Center for Women's Business Research. "Getting a very senior mentor, getting support from someone outside such as a female board member or someone the CEO and board listen to, and being a rainmaker at the highest levels are all ways to deal with it. When all else fails, make certain head hunters know you are available for a senior position—or start your own business!"

The view from Europe is important to consider in our global economy. According to Carina Bloom, marketing and operations director for the international travel trade show IMEX in Frankfurt, Germany: "Discrimination against women in the workplace is dependent upon a number of issues such as country and culture, type and size of company, and industry sector." She points out that "It is important to remember that often discrimination can be related to an individual's behavior, and it can be misleading to interpret such behavior as representative of an entire industry or office."

Are You Being Left Out of the Feast?
. . . .

It is not productive to harbor a vague feeling that you're being discriminated against or excluded because you are a woman. Instead, you need to identify *exactly* where and

---

(continued)

how this is being manifested so that you can plot your strategies to counteract sexism.

Answer these questions:

- Am I happy with my salary? Is there evidence that I would be paid more for doing this job if I were a man?
- Was I ever passed over for a promotion I deserved? Did a man get the job? Was he more qualified? Did I ask why I wasn't promoted?
- Are my ideas taken seriously?
- Am I included in meetings and shown respect during them?
- Are my projects funded up to par?
- Am I given the support staff I need? Are men at my level given more support?
- Is my office space suitable for my level?

The Big Two: Pay and Promotion

Title VII of the U.S. Civil Rights Act of 1964 prohibits discrimination in hiring, promotion, discharge, pay, fringe benefits, job training, classification, referral, and other aspects of employment, on the basis of race, color, religion, sex, or national origin. This law is enforced by the Equal Employment Opportunity Commission (EEOC), a federal agency.

If you believe you are the victim of gender discrimination that impacts on your compensation or promotion, you may decide to seek help by consulting your company's human resources department. Then, if you still feel you are not getting any results, you may need to contact the EEOC or an attorney. However, these are serious steps and may have repercussions—professional, emotional, and financial. And so they should be your last alternative.

Before you take drastic measures, consider some of the following strategies to see if you resolve the issues of disparity.

Five Steps to Fair Compensation

1. Research salaries for comparable jobs.
2. Ask your mentor and peers in other companies for advice.
3. Document your performance and results.
4. Prepare how you will ask for a raise and practice your presentation.
5. Ask for a raise in a confident tone and manner!

"If you're doing a superior job in the workplace, negotiating better pay and perks is far easier than if you're not. So make it a part of your every day responsibility to log and track your accomplishments," says Maria Brennan, executive director of American Women in Radio and Television. "When negotiating within an existing employment situation, make your case eloquently. Be confident, but not conceited; talk enough, but not too much, and be able to quantify your successes," she recommends. "And remember, people don't deserve a raise because the landlord raised the rent. People deserve more for a job well done. Always keep your negotiations germane to your workplace contributions, not mitigating factors—be it for advancement or a raise."

Promotion Tactics

If you think that you're not being promoted because you're a woman

- Do the job before you're hired to do it. Ask to take on some of the extra responsibilities involved to prove yourself.

(continued)

- Pursue any additional education that will help you get pro-moted, such as getting an MBA or advanced certification.
- Develop a polished summary of your qualifications and highlights of your achievements to back up your bid for a promotion.
- Be aware of your weaknesses and ready to answer chal-lenges to your qualifications.
- Research companies that have women's career develop-ment programs.
- Look at online sites for lists of the best companies for women.

If you're trying to overcome hurdles to promotion: "Determine your goal and then consider how men have successfully navigated their rise," suggests Laila Rach, associate dean at New York University Hotel School. "Know your strengths and issues in order to avoid any 'don't meet qualifications' pitfalls."

When you're seeking promotion, especially in the higher levels, you have to make it clear that you're committed to putting in your time. Research by Heidi Hartmann, president of the Institute for Women's Policy Research, and economist Stephen J. Rose, found that many employers assume there is a probability that women will drop out of the work force for family reasons. This exacer-bates a tendency to underinvest in women's careers and place them into dead-end jobs. If you're committed to staying in the work force full-time, make that known so that these biases are not an underlying reason for being passed up.

Above all, don't let failure discourage you from trying again and again, to reach for the brass ring. Success requires a conflu-ence of persistence and timing.

In *Sleeping Beauty,* many gallant suitors try to penetrate the briar hedge that surrounds the castle, only to get caught in the thorns and perish. But when the lucky prince comes along, the hundred-year spell is set to expire. So the thorny briars part easily and allow him to gain entry to the castle. This element of the story illustrates that timing is key when you're trying to break through barriers. There may be a particular position that no woman in your company has ever attained, but that doesn't mean you can't be the first. You might be the right woman at the right time.

Cut Through the Briar

Women can face many other forms of discrimination and exclusion outside of the major areas of pay and promotion. And these more insidious forms of discrimination can stick you like thorns and tangle you up until you lose momentum. Here are ways to cut through the briar so that you can keep moving toward the castle.

How to Have Your Ideas Taken More Seriously by Men (and Women)

- Practice delivering your ideas beforehand, preferably in front of a man who can give you feedback, or an experienced coach or woman who has worked extensively with men.
- Back up each idea by delineating what it has done or will do to move the business forward. Consider using graphs and spreadsheets, but keep them concise.
- Listen to the flow of the conversation and be judicious about finding openings. If you interrupt or insist on being heard, just be ready. Some men might perceive it as desperation.
- Evaluate communication habits that you learned long ago from parents or teachers. You may have to get out of your comfort zone to kick some ineffective habits. I find this tough to do, having been raised a nice Catholic Southern girl and taught not to step on toes. But when I stretch past these inhibitions, it is very liberating!

- If an idea you've presented has fallen flat with a boss or other decision-maker, ask for feedback from someone you trust. Perhaps it was your delivery at fault, not the idea itself, and you can hone your presentation for the next try.
- Don't take "no" for an answer. When you get a negative response, don't necessarily agree. Say, "Hmm….I'll think about that, let me get back to you; I may have a few more ideas…"
- If you're excluded at formal meetings, put your issue on the written agenda beforehand whenever possible. If men make disparaging remarks, you don't have to laugh along but don't start a big confrontation at the meeting, either. You can deal with them later. Just calmly continue to make your points.

Judy B. Rosener, professor of graduate school management at the University of California, Irvine, and author of groundbreaking books and articles on workplace gender issues, talks about an interesting phenomenon in her book *America's Competitive Secret: Women Managers.* "In the workplace, messages sent between men and women are difficult to understand because of sexual static in the air….Women are frustrated because they feel the static could be minimized if men understood gender differences. Men just want the static to go away. They feel working with women means walking on eggshells and although they're not sure what causes the static, they know it's associated with the presence of women. For this reason, men subconsciously find excuses for excluding women from the executive suite."

Get Your Fair Share of Budget and Staff

Sometimes women managers are given smaller budgets for their projects or departments, as if they are being doled out "house money" instead of being entrusted with the major financial resources. If you run into this situation, counteract it by coming to the table with well-prepared research and numbers to show why you need more money. Stick to the facts and figures instead of making an emotional plea for a bigger budget. Try to construct a justification for a higher budget that is difficult to dispute.

Both men and women feel a dearth of support staff in today's leaner corporate environment. But management tends to be even skimpier when assigning support staff to women, since in the back of many people's minds there's still a picture of a woman *in* the assistant's role.

If you feel that your lack of staff is due to sexism, prepare a strong, fact-based argument for why you require more employees. Base this presentation on how an additional staff member or two or outside contract worker will make you more effective and improve the contribution you can make to the company's bottom-line results, rather than emphasizing how put-upon and overburdened you feel. Don't say, "I can't keep up with all this paperwork…It's cutting into my productivity…I don't have time to meet with clients." Instead, frame it as a positive: "With this additional person to take care of my expense reports and paper-work, I'll be able to contact a dozen more potential clients each week and that could generate thousands in additional revenue."

A Woman's Office Is Her Castle

Office space assignments are another way in which women are sometimes subtly demeaned.

Jillian was happily ensconced in a nice office when her boss tried to pull the rug out from under her. He told her that she had to move to less appealing space to allow someone on a higher level to sit in the office she was in. Her reply was: "Then I need a promotion so I can stay here—otherwise it will look like a *demotion*." Funny thing, this offhand reply actually got Jillian's boss thinking, and soon Jillian had a big promotion.

Of course, it doesn't always work this way. Offices are territory, and men like to mark out the bigger and better spaces. Women are sometimes deemed petty if they make a big deal about their offices, so analyze if it's worth the fight before you speak up. If it is important to you, scope out what other space is available, or when it will open up. That way you can make a specific request, such as: "I'd like to move to Room 21 when Jim moves to the second floor." This type of request is harder to dismiss than a general demand for a bigger or better office.

Avoid Age Discrimination

In the Disney film *Sleeping Beauty,* the evil fairy Maleficent is quite striking and glamorous in a wicked way. But in the Charles Perrault tale, she is described as "…a very old fairy, whom they had not invited, because it was above fifty years since she had been out of a certain tower, and she was believed to be either dead or enchanted." The king figures it is safe to exclude her because she's over the hill.

In the workplace, too, age discrimination is an issue that concerns women. It is far from universal, however. I've found that it depends on both women's attitudes and the company culture. For instance, the hotel and travel industry is full of women who really take care of themselves and seem to get better with age.

There are certain industries where age discrimination against women is intractable. But in most sectors, the consensus is that appearance and attitude matter, but not necessarily age. Good looks certainly help, but they don't necessarily have to be *youthful* looks.

"The problem with age is that it is associated with lower energy levels, less creativity, not being up to date on the latest business concepts," says Sharon Hadary. "So anyone, man or woman, can counteract age concerns with staying active, projecting a high energy level, and keeping up to date and open to new ideas."

Age as an Advantage

There is, in fact, a growing trend to celebrate older people as the demographics shift. The baby boomers, with their huge economic

clout, are no longer spring chickens, and marketers are acknowl-
edging the importance of this massive customer base.

Along with many marketing executives, I embrace this trend.
And I believe in respecting older people not just as potential
customers who mean dollar signs, but as a precious resource of
wisdom and experience. I'm the youngest of four sisters (plus I
have a younger brother and three step-brothers). I'm married to
an older man, and I've had many wonderful older bosses and
mentors. I've always considered it a privilege to work with and be
with older people.

Pat Olhausen, administrative assistant at Cambrio Health
Solutions (and one of my favorite cousins) makes a good point
that many women come into their own with age. "Women often
find it hard to strike the right balance between ladylike expectations and assertiveness, especially since assertiveness is sometimes classified as aggressiveness," she says. "Luckily, with age,
women tend to become more confident—or maybe we just don't
give a darn anymore!"

I find it's a real plus to work with older people as colleagues,
since they tend not to "fake it" like a younger person might. My pet
peeve is when less experienced people overpromise and underde-
liver because they think they know it all, when, if they had just
asked more questions, the project would have been better off. So
remember, if you're just starting out: Don't be afraid to ask for
advice. Treat older people in your office as a valuable resource
instead of assuming that they are out of touch or outdated.

One manifestation of ageism I have seen is that younger
employees prefer to work for a woman who is under forty, or a
man, because they think that a woman over forty is not going to
make it to the top or inner circle to help them advance in their
careers. Don't make the mistake of discounting the importance of
older women in your organization—they can be your strongest
allies and mentors. They can also be the best sources of jobs in
new companies that offer terrific opportunities to get in on the
ground floor, since more women start new businesses than men.

Don't Bring the Curse on Your Company

Being a woman, and therefore subject to discrimination, does not make you exempt from being labeled the oppressor. Women, too, can be subject to charges of discrimination that bring a high cost to the company: expensive litigation defense, negative publicity, poor morale, and loss in clientele and revenue.

Sometimes the smallest misstep can cause a major problem. Genevieve had an impressive title, but no assistant to help her field the huge number of e-mails and phone calls she received each day. Sometimes something slipped through the cracks. This happened when she accidentally deleted an e-mail from a client, mistaking it for spam. The client took offense and thought that she was being ignored because of her ethnicity.

The client took her business to another company, and wrote a letter to the CEO of Genevieve's company accusing her of prejudice. Despite the fact that Genevieve apologized and explained that it was simply a slip-up, the client had made up her mind otherwise and the damage was done. This was particularly painful to Genevieve because she was actively involved in women's professional organizations, and believed there was a certain sisterhood among women in her industry. It's like missing the extra place setting in the Sleeping Beauty story—not an intentional slight, but a misunderstanding with serious consequences.

In a complicated and diverse workplace, there's no way to avoid every possible action that can be misconstrued as discrimination. But here are some sensible tactics for avoiding common pitfalls.

Always Have an Extra Place Setting Ready to Make Room at the Table

Treat everyone at work, of every background, with basic courtesy and respect. Ask after people's kids, dogs, and ailments, if you care. If you don't, be sincere about what you do care about: sports, music, art, NASCAR, or gardening. Find common ground with people.

If you're in a management position, pay attention to all your actions, big and small, to make sure you're giving all your staff an equal playing field. "The first thing is to take a hard look at your actions," says Colleen Lee, who is a former director of Worldwide Diversity for MCI and current board member of Women Work!, an organization dedicated to empowering women from diverse backgrounds to achieve economic self-sufficiency. "If you treat everyone fairly and don't play favorites, you stand a better chance of being viewed as someone who doesn't discriminate. Often it's the small gestures that we aren't always aware of that might make someone think we're discriminating. So, take the time to think about your actions."

Here I must say a word about white males in the workplace, who, believe it or not, sometimes feel like they are at the bottom of the totem pole. I believe in many cases they are still the ones running the show. But if you're in a supervisory role, be sure to give your nonminority male employees as much opportunity as anyone. It's only fair.

Don't beat yourself up, however, if you've tried everything to be fair and it doesn't work out perfectly. Remember the king in the story, who thought what he did was the right thing. Some people just can't be won over.

Wake Up to Other Cultures

"I believe the best way to appreciate and celebrate differences is taking the time to truly understand others," says Colleen Lee.

It's not only good business to learn about my colleagues' different cultures; it's often fun. Try these ideas:

- Once a month, ask someone to lunch who is from a different culture. You'll find they are just as curious about you as you are about them.
- Once you've gotten to know people, ask them how they prefer to be referred to culturally. Admit you feel uncomfortable but want to be educated.

- Suggest to your human resources department that your company pick a culture to celebrate once a month, with special dishes and displays that explain that culture.
- Share your American culture. Take foreign colleagues to their first American football game, Fourth of July fireworks show, or Thanksgiving dinner.

Most of us know enough to avoid remarks or actions that are overtly discriminating. But with the hypersensitive climate of today's workplace, a little *faux pas* can make the wrong impression. Be considerate of cultural sensitivities, big and small. For example, don't call a religious Jewish person late on Friday afternoon as he's getting ready to head home before the Sabbath sunset and expect a lengthy conversation. Don't go on and on about your latest attempt to lose five pounds in front of a person who has a real weight problem, or someone whose culture accepts larger women.

And please, learn how to say people's names correctly! It means a lot to everyone, but particularly for people from other cultures; learning to pronounce their names is an important sign of respect. And respect, along with opportunity, is the soul of inclusion.

Support Multicultural Initiatives

Become actively involved in diversity initiatives both inside your company and in other professional organizations, and make your support known. Supporting people of various cultures is not only the right moral choice; it is the smart way to do business. Remember that when Sleeping Beauty is pricked by the needle, not only does *she* fall asleep—the entire court goes into a dormant state! Excluding the fairy has a ripple effect, causing everyone and everything in the palace to stop dead in their tracks.

Similarly, in the twenty-first century a business cannot evolve and prosper without embracing multiculturalism. Thirteen million out of 44 million American workers were members of minorities according to the 2000 census, and the numbers keep growing. This is a human resource that no company can afford to underutilize.

Nonetheless, if you champion a diversity initiative—or a woman's initiative—you may experience a backlash. Some people will worry that the company is no longer going to reward their efforts if they are not minority employees. Some will think that these programs mean preferential treatment for certain groups. Diversity and women's initiatives often have an impact akin to a merger or acquisition, where everyone is scrambling with a new culture and shifting positions. These changes bring out both the best and worst in people. That's when you have to keep the faith.

"I would encourage women to keep holding on to what is right, true, and just," says Faye Jackson, executive director of the Hospitality Industry Diversity Institute. "Even in the midst of adversity, I would encourage women to remember there is joy, there is hope, and there can be peace."

Don't get entangled in rumors, fear-mongering, and office intrigues related to diversity issues. These factors tend to level out if you hold yourself above them. Stay strong in your commitment to see that *all* the people in your organization have an opportunity to wake up to their full potential.

....

Sleeping Beauty Shows Them All

Once upon a time, about 30 years ago, a baby girl named Aurora was born to parents who treated her like a princess from day one. The parents planned a lavish christening party under a white tent on the manicured lawn of their palatial neo-Tudor home. They invited all their neighbors except a reclusive old man who nobody liked because he let his lawn and his hedges grow wild.

At the christening party, the well-heeled guests raised crystal goblets of champagne to toast the baby girl.

"I wish her beauty," said the first guest, an aging homecoming queen who still clung to the hairstyle of her youth.

"I wish that she marry a rich man who adores her," said a wealthy older man's trophy wife.

"I wish that she become a good tennis player," said the third guest, a country club champion, who sported a year-round suntan.

"I wish that she have perfect pitch," said the local piano teacher, who saw a lucrative future pupil in the sleeping baby.

"I wish that she get straight A's, and go to a good college," said the fifth, who was dismayed by the superficiality of the other toasts.

"I wish that she become a caring person, who never forgets those less fortunate," said the sixth guest, a lady who chaired charity balls.

"I wish her an interesting career," said the seventh, the only woman in the neighborhood who had bought her own house.

Just then the party was interrupted by the arrival of the old man with the shabby property, who figured it was an open tent and he'd wander in for some free chow. He bellowed: "And I wish that she learn that a woman's place is in the home!" Then he grabbed a handful of jumbo shrimp off a silver tray and stuffed them in his mouth.

The girl's aunt nudged the mean old man aside. "I am Aurora's godmother," she said. "And I wish that she grow up to realize that women can do just about anything they set out to do, no matter what anyone says."

The years passed and Aurora grew up to be a kind and accomplished young woman.

After graduating with a degree in marketing, she went to work for a large company, the biggest manufacturer of mattresses in the world.

Innocent as she was, she didn't realize it was a danger sign that this company had no women in senior management. Men of middling ability were promoted as women languished in dead-end positions. And those women who bravely bid for promotion were unable to break through the thicket of ingrained sexism that permeated the firm. It was clear to Aurora, with her business degree, that the whole company suffered from this ossified corporate mindset. Yet she decided to stick it out for a year to build her résumé.

The days dragged by, and it seemed to Aurora that she had been stuck there a hundred years. Then a poor earnings report compelled the company to seek out the advice of consultants. They recommended that the corporation institute programs to develop women for leadership positions. Since it was women who made most mattress-buying decisions, their perspective was crucial in the upper echelons of the company.

Aurora signed up for the women's mentoring and networking initiative the day it was launched. When she and other women were promoted six months later, a breeze of fresh talent swept through the company, clearing away the bramble of corporate stagnation to make way for increased profits.

And Aurora worked there happily ever after, at least until she was offered a bigger opportunity at an upscale home furnishing firm. After all, there was a bigger world out there than just mattresses.

....

Fairy Dust from *Sleeping Beauty*

- If you're seeking a promotion or raise, do a superior job and track your accomplishments on a daily basis.
- Take on some of the tasks associated with the job you want before you're promoted to prove yourself.
- Keep trying until you hit the right opportunity at the right time. Success requires both persistence and timing.
- Appearance and attitude matter in the workplace, not necessarily age. Keep your energy up and your ideas fresh.
- Treat everyone with consideration and don't play favorites if you want a reputation as someone who doesn't discriminate.
- Be aware of small gestures and slip-ups that might be misconstrued. Learn about coworkers' different cultures—and learn how to pronounce their names!
- The whole company will stagnate and suffer if it is not inclusive. Support diversity initiatives and be steadfast in your commitment.

CHAPTER 8

··

The Red Shoes

Keep Your Work Life from Spinning out of Control

IN THIS TRAGIC HANS CHRISTIAN ANDERSEN TALE, A GIRL GETS A PAIR of coveted red shoes, but finds that they have a merciless will of their own. Compelled by the shoes to dance day and night, the desperate girl finally begs the executioner to chop off her feet. This haunting image of being danced nearly to death resonates deeply with many exhausted career women.

Sometimes it seems as if we are being punished for daring to pursue the dance of an ambitious career. We deal with work overload, tough deadlines, staff shortages, and intense pressure to show results. Then, once we leave work (which is rarely at the stroke of 5 P.M.) many of us face the second shift: home and family responsibilities. We are as worn out as the girl whose red shoes keep her dancing this way and that, day and night.

Since the tragic figure in *The Red Shoes* is called Karen, there is speculation that she is named after Andersen's illegitimate half-sister, Karen Marie. The real Karen lived a life of poverty and may have worked as a prostitute for a time before she died in 1846, only a year after the Andersen story was published.

Here is a synopsis of the sorrowful tale.

A poor orphan named Karen, who has been taken in by an old lady, sees a princess wearing a pair of beautiful red shoes. When it is time for her confirmation, Karen gets a pair of red shoes from the shoemaker and wears them to church. When the old lady finds out, she forbids Karen to wear the red shoes to church ever again, but the vain girl disobeys. A crippled soldier outside the church taps her feet and says: "See what beautiful dancing shoes! Mind you stick fast when you dance."

The old lady becomes ill and Karen is supposed to nurse her, but she leaves her duty to put on the red shoes and dance at a ball. The shoes seem to take on a life of their own, and they dance her away into the dark forest. They stick to her feet and she is forced to dance day and night. At the church she sees an angel who says, "You shall dance in your red shoes till your skin shrivels up and you are a skeleton..." Finally Karen begs an executioner to cut off her feet to get rid of the shoes. When he does, the bedeviled shoes dance away on their own.

Karen, now crippled and repentant, finds refuge in the home of a parson and his wife. One Sunday the angel appears and spirits Karen back to church, her sins forgiven. Her heart breaks with joy and her soul flies up to heaven, where no one asks about the red shoes.

The Red Shoes is a stern religious tale that imparts a dire warning against the sin of vanity. But we can also find in it a more relevant message about the danger of pursuing what we love relentlessly, without heed to consequences. There is also the lesson that what we fear (job failure or financial woes) can drive us to dance after the unattainable.

Two of England's greatest postwar filmmakers, Michael Powell and Emeric Pressburger explored the deeper themes of the tale in their melodramatic film *The Red Shoes* (1948). The central plot tells the story of a flame-haired ballerina who has to choose between her ambition and her love for a young composer. (The movie also features a 15-minute ballet version of the Hans

Christian Andersen tale that is one of the most fantastic dance sequences ever put on film!)

Alas, for most of us the choices are not so glamorous. We don't get to decide between a glorious dance career and a blissful marriage to a dashing composer. In fact, the very notion of choosing *between* career and marriage is outmoded. Now, we expect to have both a satisfying personal life and a rewarding career.

And even if we might *want* to give up our career for the joys of homemaking, we usually *need* to keep working. It is not necessarily about choice or fulfillment. Economics can be a huge factor. We have to keep dancing to pay the bills.

Giving up is not an option. So we have to learn to keep our work from spinning out of control, to delegate, negotiate, and sometimes say "no." We must look for creative ways to balance our personal and professional priorities. We need to lead the dance of our careers in the direction we desire.

Delegate, Negotiate, and Know When to Say "No"

"The shoes would not let her do what she liked…When she wanted to dance up the room, the shoes danced down the room, and then down the stairs, through the streets, and out of the town gate. Away she danced, and away she had to dance, right away into the dark forest…" the fairy tale goes—and so does reality.

Sometimes it seems as if our work takes on a will of its own, leading the dance. The work piles up and our days spin out of control. We can't get back in charge, can't take control—unless we master the key skills of delegation and drawing the line when we need to say "no."

Bridge the Barriers to Delegation

Delegation is a core competence for women who want to manage their workloads. But it doesn't always come naturally. Determine which of these barriers might be keeping you from effective delegation, and learn how to get around them.

You think you can do it better. Maybe you are the best. But does this task really demand your level of expertise? Can someone else do it sufficiently, if not quite as splendidly as you?

You think you can do it faster. It's probably true. But you still have limited time and there is probably something with a bigger payoff that you could be doing instead.

You think that it will take longer to teach someone else to do it than to do it yourself. This may be true initially. But if you invest a little time in training someone else to do the task and it becomes his regular responsibility, it will save you a lot of time in the long run.

You think you'll look bad with your boss if you let someone else do it. This is rarely the reality. People in higher positions know how to delegate, and you'll gain status in their eyes if you demonstrate mastery of this management skill.

You think you won't be seen as indispensable if you delegate. Relinquishing one or two tasks is not going to devalue you. Instead, higher-ups will get accustomed to the idea of having you concentrate on more significant work, and will assign routine tasks to someone else.

You're afraid the person to whom you delegate will take your job. Maybe that person will—when you get promoted. Delegation will free up your time for work that requires more talent and experience, paving the way to promotion.

Delegation Planner
• •

Write down a list of the tasks you perform at work. Designate each one Level 1, 2, or 3.

(continued)

Level 1: Tasks that you are sure no one else can do

Level 2: Tasks that someone else can do with additional training or help

Level 3: Tasks that someone else can do without training

Next to each Level 3 task, write down someone to whom you might delegate the job.

Next to each Level 2 task, list a suitable candidate and what training that person will need.

Delegating Versus Dumping

In today's harried work environment, it's important to be sensitive to the difference between delegating effectively and just dumping work on someone else.

Dumping is when you pass on the job without due consideration of the person's skills, experience, or time availability. Delegating entails speaking to the person to confirm that she has the required skills, and, if not, determining how she can get additional training or guidance.

Time availability is a tricky issue, since everyone feels pressed, and if you ask: "Do you have the time to do this?" the answer is likely to be "Not really." A more productive approach is to inquire, "How can you fit this into your schedule?" If the answer is negative, help the person to determine what else he might delegate or set aside to make time for the new responsibility.

Provide your team member with the following information:

- The ultimate goal of the task or project
- The steps to achieve the goal
- The deadline
- Resources for support and information

Motivating

For delegation to be successful in the long run, you have to inspire and motivate the people to whom you delegate. First, make it clear you have confidence in your team member's abilities. Next, let the person know that you're there if needed along the way (although you're quite certain that the person can handle the job). Explain sufficiently, but don't micromanage. Let someone else be the hero.

When the task is completed, make an effort to be encouraging even if it wasn't done as fast or well as you hoped. And try not to "de-delegate" or take the work back on your plate too quickly. Instead, figure out how you can bring the person up to speed.

Money and promotion talk, so if you're in a position of power, let it be known that there are rewards waiting in the wings for those who excel. If you can't directly reward the person to whom you delegated a certain task, put in a good word with higher-ups.

"By talking continuously with my staff, maintaining a daily presence, and praising work well done, my staff stays motivated," says Ray Bloom, CEO of the international travel trade show IMEX. "By giving levels of responsibility appropriate to ability, people are able to take real ownership and pride in their work. Every single member of the team is regarded as a true asset and contributor to the overall success of the company, and this atmosphere breeds motivation."

When There Is Nowhere to Turn

Corporations are running lean and mean, and many are understaffed. You may not have any support staff available for delegation. When this is the case, consider delegating to your peers—but be careful about stepping on toes by calling it delegation. "Teamwork" is a more tactful term that doesn't smack of hierarchy.

If peers are unavailable, inquire if there is room in the budget for a temporary employee or an outside consultant. If not, you have two choices:

1. Delegate the work to a future date (next week, next month or next week), or
2. Prepare to explain to your boss why you do not have the time or resources to do it.

The Art of Saying "No"

When I was young, every nice girl was taught to say "no" when boys got fresh. Too bad nobody ever taught us to how to say "no" to work overload! It makes sense to decline when we don't have the time or skill to do the job justice. So why do we find it is so tough?

Women feel they have to outperform men. It's not enough to do as well as men at work. We have to do better, faster, and more. And so we feel we have to take on whatever challenges are presented. But there is a difference between stretching yourself and overloading. Before you agree to do something, take a few minutes to think about it. Make sure that you have a reasonable chance of success and that you have sufficient time to do your best.

Women want to please. Typically, we women believe we will be valued more if we please others. And what better way to please than to say: "Sure, I'll take care of that for you." Well, you can't please all the people all the time. If you take on everything, you'll end up disappointing others and driving yourself over the brink.

Women want to be positive. We all want to be seen as upbeat, can-do women (especially we former cheerleader types). But you have to balance optimism with reality. Yes, take risks, stretch, go for the gold. But don't take on so much that you drive yourself to exhaustion. Don't raise the bar so high that you have no chance of making it over in one piece. Going beyond what you told people to expect is better than failing to deliver what you promise.

"I really have no problem in saying 'no,' as long as I do it in a positive way and offer a thoughtful and meaningful reason," says Colleen Barrett, president of Southwest Airlines. "Southwest, and I personally, have never held out the hope that we could be all things for all people. We have traditionally underpromised and overdelivered."

How to Say No Without Being a Naysayer

- Avoid flying off the handle and remain calm.
- Say that you would like to do it, but you lack the time.
- If time is the issue, explain the other priorities that are filling your hours.
- Consider when you might be able to take on the task or project in the future.
- If the problem is that you lack the skills, ask if you could get additional training.
- If the task or project is something you've done in the past but don't have time to do now, offer to write down instructions or coach someone else.

Reasons to Say "No"

If you find yourself saying "no" too often at work, step back to look at underlying reasons.

Your company or department is understaffed. It could be that management is expecting more than is humanly possible from the people who are left after downsizing. If this is the case, review your job description carefully. Then talk to your boss about planning a daily or weekly priority list together so you can always accomplish what's most important.

You're bored with your job. Another scenario is that you're saying "no" because you're blasé about your job. Perhaps it's become too routine and easy. To counteract this malaise, seek out projects that are more demanding and thought-provoking, yet still within your capabilities.

You're turned off by your coworkers. Sometimes it's the people you're working with who are the problem. I know that if I'm approached by someone who has the habit of dropping the ball (on me), I'm less likely to willingly sign on. When this happens, see if you can bring someone else on to the team to "psych you up" for the project.

You're a wonder-woman. It could be that you have such a fantastic reputation that people think you can pull off anything. This puts you in the catbird's seat to ask for a raise and a promotion.

Negotiating Principles

- Be realistic (not inflated or too modest) about how much value you bring to the company.
- Know how much power the person with whom you're negotiating has to grant your request.
- Ask questions and get information from the other side.
- Know in advance what you're willing to compromise and concede.
- Successful negotiation is a process of reciprocity. Be willing to offer something of value in return for what you want.
- If your bosses are not willing to give you what you want, find out what they are willing to give.
- After you agree to terms verbally, ask for a follow-up agreement in writing.

Don't assume that management will take the initiative to compensate you for going the extra mile. More likely, you'll have to ask for what you deserve. If you think you can't get the most for yourself, ask a mentor to advocate or negotiate for you.

Another choice is to negotiate for something other than a promotion or pay increase. This could be the time to ask for an assistant, a bigger budget for your department, the go-ahead on a pet project, a better office space, or an alternative work arrangement such as different hours or working from home. Seize the moment when you're the "golden girl" and go for it!

The Balancing Point

Picture the ballerina in the film version of *The Red Shoes*. She balances in an *arabesque en pointe* for only a brief, thrilling moment before she transitions into another step. Even the most talented ballerina cannot stay perfectly balanced for very long. And neither can any woman who is trying to balance work and family. Balancing personal and professional priorities requires constant adjustment, flexibility, and compromise.

"You can set priorities between demands of work and family, but as a daily routine, balance or equity are impossible to achieve," says Irma Mann, owner of Irma Inc (a research and marketing firm) and former VP for Sonesta Hotels. "I think it's time for women to erase 'balance' as a goal. Do we pay attention to business and love our families? Of course we do. But can we *balance* this everyday—no. Can we *manage* it every day? Yes."

Work/family balance is a highly individual process, with so many variables that I wouldn't presume to give you a one-size-fits-all solution. The only universal truth is that there is no such thing as perfect balance, especially if you work full-time and have young children. Don't fall into the trap of thinking that women who are more organized, energetic, or accomplished than you manage to have it all without guilt or stress. Don't beat yourself up if you can't maintain the ideal balance. As long as you love your kids and do the best you can, you have the right to be proud.

"I've learned that I can only do the best I can do. I have learned not to set unrealistic expectations. My 10-year-old may say, 'Mommy, do you promise to come to all my soccer games this year?' My realistic response is, 'I promise to do my absolute best.' Hopefully that will be all her games. But if it's not, my daughter doesn't feel disappointed, and I don't feel guilty for letting her down," says Maria Brennan, executive director of American Women in Radio and Television. "Noting that, job number one in my life is my family and after more than 20 years in my business and ten years as a mom, I learned that means making sacrifices at the workplace. It means 'no' has become a part of my work vocabulary."

In 2003, the Women's Leadership Initiative of Meetings Professional International (MPI) published a major survey that found that the number one challenge for women who aspired to leadership positions was balancing professional responsibilities with home/family management. Women also reported the need to "hide" family issues and schedule conflicts for fear of losing their jobs or trust from their superiors or colleagues.

It is common knowledge that in two-career families, women usually take on the lion's share of responsibility for children. But the burden is exponential for single mothers.

"By hook or crook you do what you can, when you can. The gadgets help, especially a laptop computer with at-home access to work-related sites and servers," says Mary Kenner, communications advisor, retirement plans, for FedEx Corporation. "The reality is that being a single mom can't get in the way of doing the job well. And being the breadwinner can help you stay on target. You've got to bring home the bacon when it's all said and done."

Much of the conversation about women's "choices" regarding how they divide their time between family life and work skates around this big piece of the puzzle: It's not just that we *want* to work; we also *need* to work. New York University's hotel school market research found that 40 percent of women business travelers are sole or primary earners.

Money is a family priority, too, and sometimes it conflicts with other priorities, causing fear-based actions and guilty feelings.

Joyce had to take an important business trip to give a major presentation. But her child's class play was during the week she would be away. Her family was her first priority, but they needed her income, and missing the business trip would jeopardize her job. Joyce had to embark on her business trip with that sinking feeling so familiar to working moms: No matter what she did, it seemed like the wrong choice.

Working mother's guilt is a complex issue, and there are no simple solutions. But it might help to look at it from a historical perspective. The image of mother waiting at the front door with milk and cookies after school, ready to give her children doting attention for the rest of the day, is largely a mid-20th-century TV sitcom fantasy. Before the advent of washing machines, prepared foods and other modern conveniences, women were consumed with work: growing food, canning, cooking, sewing, washing, and cleaning. Often, mothers worked outside in the fields much of the day and young children were cared for by relatives or neighbors— or the kids worked, too!

There is nothing new or unnatural about a mother who is busy working. Children have always been able to thrive if they know they are loved, regardless of whether their mother is working or not.

Kids are born with their own personalities and predilections. If your child is having a problem, of course you want to do everything you can to fix it. But don't blame your career. Children whose mothers work full-time can be happy and well-adjusted, while those with stay-at-home moms (or dads) sometimes have emotional issues—and vice-versa. Giving up your career won't necessarily fix everything. As long as you love your children and provide them with the best care you can, you don't deserve the burden of guilt if things aren't perfect.

Alternative Work Arrangements

Many working women—moms and otherwise—look to alternative work arrangements as a means of achieving more balance in their lives. Certain fields are more conducive to these arrangements: sales, real estate, accounting, bookkeeping, and creative work such as writing, graphic arts, Web design, and so on. But many women also manage to incorporate alternative work arrangements into jobs that are traditionally 9-to-5 positions.

There are several different ways you can reconfigure your work week while still staying employed (rather than starting your own business, which is another possibility). Each of these arrangements has pros and cons that should be weighed before you propose them to your company. And changing, evolving economic times dictate options sometimes more than not.

Also, be aware that high-level people in the company have to be a visible, present force in order to lead and inspire. So if your goal is to become a VP or CEO, alternative work arrangements might hinder your advancement. But if your vision of success has more to do with freedom and family, consider the options.

Part-Time Employment

Working part-time is a great way to keep your career going while still having lots of time to spend with your children—provided you have another source of income. You'll need a husband, partner, trust fund, or fairy godmother to fill in the gaps, since very few people can live well in today's pricey world on a part-time salary.

Besides the monetary disadvantage, there are a few other issues with part-time work. You may miss the chance to participate in important projects and be out of the office when critical decisions are made. Over time, you may lose key alliances with coworkers and bosses, have less credibility, and get passed up for promotion—unless you're ready to return to full-time status.

Job Sharing

In job-sharing arrangements, two employees work part-time, each performing half of one full-time job. Job-sharing is one of those utopian ideas that sounds great on paper but is fraught with pitfalls in reality, which is why you don't hear of too many people doing it. The biggest hurdle is finding a partner who has the right set of skills and is content with the allotted hours and half a salary. You must be able to communicate well, trust the other person to follow through, and respect each other's judgment. Job-sharing works best in support- and mid-level jobs in which the tasks are clearly defined and reasonably contained. For upper-level positions it is rarely an option.

Flex Time and Compressed Work Week

Flex time means that you work the same number of hours per day as a standard schedule, but you start or finish earlier or later than the usual 9 to 5 hours (for example, you work 7 to 3 or 10:30 to 6:30). This might allow you to avoid rush hour traffic, take your child to an afternoon karate class, or put your kids on the school bus in the morning before work.

Ten Ways to Sell an Alternative Work Arrangement to Your Employer
....

1. Wait until you've been at the company long enough to prove yourself.
2. Be specific about what you're proposing.
3. Focus on the benefits to the company, not to you.
4. Explain how you'll structure your work load.

(continued)

5. Detail how you will stay in touch.
6. Offer some added value to your company in return.
7. Tell your boss that you will be flexible about coming in for important meetings, even if they fall on your telecommuting days.
8. If you're asking to work at home, explain how you will set up your office and who will pay for the equipment and connections that you will require.
9. Allow a review time for your alternative work arrangement proposal. Pushing for a quick answer might result in a negative response.
10. Suggest a trial period, after which you and your employer can evaluate how the arrangement is working.

According to Ellen Galinsky, president of the Families and Work Institute, flex time programs have increased 14 percent over the last decade and are available at 68 percent of all companies. Despite this widespread accommodation, some employers might be put off by the term "flex time" and misconstrue it to mean that you can come and go as you please, which is the very antithesis of the corporate work ethic. You can avoid this misconception by simply requesting a change in your regular work hours instead of calling it flex time.

Another alternative to the Monday through Friday grind is the compressed work week, in which you put in your 35 or 40 hours in a different configuration. For example, you might work ten hours a day four days a week. This is usually less popular with employers, who suspect that your energy will lag during a ten-hour shift, or who just want you available every day.

Telecommuting

Telecommuting can mean any arrangement in which you spend some of your time working at home. The main advantage is that you avoid commuting hours, which can be a huge drain. Plus, you don't have to bother with suitable office attire (although you probably won't feel as competent if you work in your pajamas and fuzzy slippers).

Despite its obvious appeal, there are some drawbacks to telecommuting full-time. You might be able to participate in meetings via conference calls, but at times it can be awkward. Your relationships with your coworkers might suffer because they're jealous of your freedom, or they think that you're sloughing off at home. Your boss might also harbor resentment, even if she or he agreed to the arrangement. However, if you are showing good results for the company, these issues might be mitigated.

Telecommuting part-time can allow you to have the best of both worlds. An arrangement where you work at home one or two days a week enables you to maintain a visible presence at the office, yet still enjoy a break from the daily commute.

If your employer accepts the idea, it is *your* responsibility to make sure that your telecommuting arrangement goes smoothly. This means setting up a separate phone line and a quiet office space where you give an impression of absolute professionalism. Be certain that you can have uninterrupted phone conversations without any distracting noises in the background. An occasional barking dog might slide by, but raucous cartoons or "tweeny" pop music won't do.

Don't imagine that your baby will be gurgling happily in the corner of your office, or that your toddler will be quietly playing with blocks while you concentrate on your telecommuting job. If you want to be focused and productive, you'll need childcare, even if that means a babysitter watching your children in another room while you're in your home office.

Make a point of responding to e-mails and phone calls quickly on your at-home days, so that everyone at the office feels you're in touch. And even if you're given permission to telecommute full-time, stop by the office as frequently as you can. There is simply no replacement for face time.

Business Travel in the Right Direction

"So off she danced, and off she had to dance, over fields and meadows, in rain and sunshine, by day and by night, but at night it was fearful," goes an evocative passage in *The Red Shoes*.

Business travel can make us feel that we're working day and night, and can be a particularly stressful part of the professional life. But there are resourceful ways to turn business travel into an opportunity for rejuvenation. Try these tips to make your travel easier and more pleasurable:

- Pre-book every leg of the trip, including airport pickup and delivery.
- Check the Internet for travel conditions in your destination city so you can select the proper clothes.
- Wrap clothes in plastic to prevent wrinkling.
- Keep small sizes of all your essential toiletries in a travel case between trips, so you don't forget anything.
- Be sure all your luggage has wheels and straps.
- With airport security delays, it's sometimes easier to check your baggage than to lug it around and carry it all on. You might also consider sending baggage FedEx or UPS (just be sure to get a tracking number).
- Leave an extra cell phone charger in your luggage if you travel frequently; otherwise it's too easy to leave the charger behind.
- Wear comfortable clothes and shoes while traveling, but be prepared to run into a client or CEO.
- Drink plenty of water before the plane trip, and take a healthy snack and water onto the plane.
- Consider bringing your favorite music with earphones, a book, or DVD to relax on the plane or in the hotel.
- Stretch before getting onto the plane and afterwards, as soon as you settle into your hotel.
- Take an exercise DVD along or rent one for an in-room workout.

- If you're pressed for time, consider foregoing a lengthy restaurant dinner in favor of a visit to the spa. Order a light room service meal afterwards.
- Book some recreation with colleagues or clients: a show or visit to a museum, a round of golf, or a shopping expedition.
- If possible, add on an extra day to rest, enjoy the facilities and locale, or see an old friend.

Many people may believe that women don't like to be wrenched away from home and hearth. But New York University surveys have uncovered an interesting secret: Women actually enjoy business travel *more* than men, and *like* getting away from home responsibilities. Most women view business travel as a positive experience overall. Eighty percent consider business travel to be a sign of professional achievement, and the majority would continue to travel for business if they had the choice.

Most women opt not to take their children on business trips. But some fearless moms find a way to combine quality family time and travel.

Patricia "Pat" Schroeder is now president and chief executive officer of the Association of American Publishers (AAP), the national trade organization of the U.S. book publishing industry. Before that, she was a popular and undefeated congresswoman, representing Colorado's First Congressional District (Denver) in the U.S. House of Representatives for twenty-four years. The mother of two young children at the time she was elected to the House, Mrs. Schroeder went on to serve twelve terms. She is a tireless advocate for children's and women's issues—and she lives her ideals.

"Having been elected in 1972 with a two- and six-year-old, work and family issues were my main legislative focus," says Pat Schroeder. "From a personal (not legislative) perspective, I was very fortunate to have children who loved to travel. They were in public school. We put the equivalent of private school tuition in the bank for them to travel with [us] but said if their grades ever fell, they would have to go to private school and there wasn't money for travel. They traveled the world with me, got great grades and went on to Princeton, Georgetown, Columbia, and Cambridge University. So travel as a bribe was a great way to go. I never had to be the bad cop and the experiences we all shared as a family were priceless."

Sixty-five percent of women incorporate some relaxing or fun activities into their business trips. Presumably many of these same women rarely have a chance for "me time" when they're back at home, swept up in their busy routines. Business travel gives them an opportunity to kick off the red shoes and get a good foot massage.

....

The Red Shoes—and Matching Suit

Karen's parents were immigrants who struggled to make a living in a tiny shoe repair shop. Every day after school, little Karen would play with her toys behind the counter. One day she looked up and saw a tall woman in a beautiful red suit with big shoulder pads. The woman held up a shiny red patent leather pump with a broken heel. "Can you fix it right away?" she asked Karen's mother. "I have to get to the airport for a business trip."

When the lady left, Karen turned to her mother and asked: "Can I be a businesswoman when I grow up? And have a red suit like that, and go on business trips?"

"If you study hard," said her mother.

And so Karen did study hard, and she was the first person in her family to go to college.

She even went on to pursue an MBA while working full-time.

Although Karen put in long hours, she was young and still had the energy to go out dancing after work. She met a man and married, but barely paused for a honeymoon, so intent was she on climbing the corporate ladder. At work, Karen became known for her meticulous attention to detail, her perfectionism, and drive. Her assistants muttered that she micromanaged, but Karen was too busy to notice these ripples of discontent.

Karen wanted it all, so she had two babies in three years. She was back at her desk exactly three weeks after each delivery. After the second baby, she wanted live-in help and a bigger house. Karen insisted that they buy the biggest house in the best neighborhood, with the heftiest mortgage they could swing. Her husband warned her that they were overreaching, but Karen scoffed at his caution.

Now it was more important than ever that Karen keep getting promotions and bigger paychecks, and so she took on more demanding projects. She never said no, even if it meant working through lunch, working at night, working on weekends.

Her mother worried that Karen was getting too thin, but Karen just laughed at the idea. "You can never be too thin or too rich, Ma," she said, proud of fitting into her wardrobe of size-two red suits.

When her children learned to talk, they said they wanted more time with Mommy. But Karen explained that Mommy had important work to do. Then she scolded the nanny for not keeping the kids content.

And so Karen kept working, longer and longer hours, her eye on a VP position. When it went to someone else, she was devastated. "Why was I passed up?" she cried to her boss. "I work so hard. I put in more hours than anyone!"

"Once you reach a certain level, it's not about clocking hours. And it's not just about what you can do. It is about what you can motivate other people to do," said her boss. "To be frank, you're lacking in delegation skills and you don't inspire your team. And you might as well know that some people find you off-putting on an interpersonal level, as well. I don't know…maybe it's those red power suits you're always wearing."

Karen went home, kicked off her shiny red pumps, and threw herself across her bed. "I work day and night for this company and look how they treat me," she cried. "I've had it. I want out!"

"You can't quit now," said her husband. "You're the one who insisted that we buy this huge house. We're mortgaged to the hilt. I can't pay for all this while you stay home and bake brownies. You wanted this house—you better keep working for it!"

Karen wept into her pillow. Yet she knew he was right. She couldn't stop now, and she didn't want to. She loved working and would be bored to death staying home—not that they could afford it, anyway.

But she could make some changes. She would look for a mentor or coach to teach her how to delegate and motivate. And talk to a business fashion consultant about how to integrate other colors (including black and white) into her day-to-day wardrobe, while keeping red as her signature color for presentations. Maybe she would make arrangements to bring her husband, nanny, and kids on a business conference getaway to Florida or the Caribbean—or even New York, where the children could learn how Mommy balanced family with work. And she'd do something to reduce her own stress level. She had always wanted to take salsa lessons…

Fairy Dust from *The Red Shoes*

- Delegating is worthwhile, even if you can do the task faster or better.
- Delegating will make you more valuable to your company, not less.
- Don't be afraid to say "no" if you don't have the time to deliver what is needed.
- When you negotiate, know in advance how much you're willing to compromise. Offer something of value in return for what you want.
- Balancing personal and professional priorities requires constant adjustment. No one can hold the perfect balance for long.
- Working moms do not have to feel guilty. Money is a family priority, too.

- Alternative work arrangements give you more freedom and family time, but at a price if you're ambitious.
- Pace yourself. You can't work constantly. Strive to be a well-rounded, healthy person rather than a one-sided, one-dimensional workaholic.
- When you're proposing an alternative arrangement to your employer, focus on the benefits to the company, not to you.
- With clever planning, you can build in time for yourself and make business travel a pleasure.

CHAPTER 9

···

Rapunzel

Share Your Ideas and Passion, and Make Your Voice Heard

IN A GREEDY ATTEMPT TO KEEP RAPUNZEL TO HERSELF, THE WITCH locks her up in a tower—and ends up losing the girl she treasures. This teaches us that it is essential to share what we know and love.

From a business standpoint, some people labor under the misguided notion that they will safeguard their position by withholding information, contacts, or assistance. But in today's interconnected work world, the collaborative approach is infinitely wiser.

Relationships are a survival tool. Collaboration and networking are key to long-range career success. Sharing provides the best opportunity to make a contribution to the company—and to the world beyond the office towers.

Everyone remembers the ladder Rapunzel fashions from her long blonde hair. But when you read the original fairy tale, you'll notice that Rapunzel actually finds her way down from the tower and, eventually, to a happy ending, through the power of her *voice*. The prince hears her singing and falls in love with her voice—not her golden tresses. Although the "golden stair" of her hair is a poetic detail that stays in our minds, the true meaning of the fairy tale lies elsewhere.

One of its primary lessons is that we must *make ourselves heard* to escape limitations. Translating this from the personal to the professional, in the work world we need to make our voices heard both on an individual basis, and on a collective level via women's professional organizations, philanthropies, and social and political activism.

The name Rapunzel comes from rampion, a leafy plant used in winter salads. And this detail gives us clues to the story's history. Like many fairy tales, the Rapunzel narrative as we know it today is a rich mix of oral and literary tales. It has literary antecedents in a Giambattista Basile story published in 1637 about a girl named Petrosinella, a name derived from *petrosine,* or parsley (a similar plant to rampion). In 1697 a French aristocrat, Charlotte Rose de Caumont de la Force, published "Persinette," in a name stemming from "persil" or parsley.

Modern thinkers have been intrigued by the symbolism in Rapunzel and subjected the story to many interpretations. Bruno Bettleheim analyzed the tale in *The Uses of Enchantment,* and the feminist poet Anne Sexton included a provocative "Rapunzel" poem in *Transformations.* Other treatments are as diverse as a serious opera in six acts by Lou Harrison—and a "Barbie as Rapunzel" video and line of merchandise!

Still, it is the simple version recorded by the Brothers Grimm that resonates through the ages with young and old. Here is the synopsis of that tale:

A pregnant woman has an intense craving for rampion (or rapunzel) that she sees growing in a garden next door. Her husband steals some for her but is caught by the witch (also called Mother Gothel) who lives there. He promises the witch their first-born child in exchange for his freedom. When the baby is born, the witch takes her away and names her Rapunzel. When Rapunzel is twelve years old, the witch locks her up in a tower with no stairs or doors. When the witch wants to come up and visit, she calls: "Rapunzel, Rapunzel, let down your hair!" and climbs up the girl's golden braids.

A prince passing by hears Rapunzel singing and falls in love with her voice. He visits her secretly and they plan her escape. But the witch finds out and is enraged. She cuts off Rapunzel's hair, and sends her away to live in the wilderness in poverty. Then the witch uses Rapunzel's shorn hair to trick the prince into coming up into the tower. When she tells him that Rapunzel is lost to him forever, he jumps out of the window in despair and is blinded by thorns. Years later, the prince hears Rapunzel's voice in the wilderness. They are reunited, and as her tears fall upon his eyes, his sight is restored.

The witch locks Rapunzel in a tower when she is twelve, the age of puberty, presumably to keep her from being seduced away by a man. She wants to keep the girl, who is the only thing she has ever loved, to herself. "I thought I separated you from all the world and yet you have deceived me," she says, when she finds out that Rapunzel has managed to meet the young prince despite her seclusion. And in her rage, she casts away the girl she cherishes and loses her forever.

Withholding, controlling witches at work can be male or female, young or old, bosses or coworkers. They are stingy about sharing their contacts, information, expertise, and help. They believe that imparting knowledge and skills will somehow weaken their position or power. And they fear that by helping others they will somehow lose out.

This attitude is as foolhardy as the witch's attempt to lock away Rapunzel. Sharing information at work is not only visionary, it is good business. Nobody gets ahead in their career by locking up their information and withholding open communication or help. (I know there is some information that just can't be shared because of rules and regulations, but you know the difference.)

Sharing knowledge through collaboration is the best way to gain respect and allies at work and be seen as a leader.

Beware of Witholding Witches

Bosses who have integrity and genuine leadership qualities will encourage you to grow in your responsibilities and position, even if it means that eventually you'll move on to a different department or company. But occasionally you might run into a boss who—subconsciously or not—doesn't want you to move on and sabotages your chances.

Gloria was an intelligent, competent legal secretary working in a large corporate law firm. Her boss, Nathan, respected and appreciated her work and they enjoyed a good working relationship. Since they were friendly, Gloria was open with Nathan about wanting to move up to a paralegal position in the firm. She also listed Nathan as her first reference because she assumed he would give her glowing reviews. But to Gloria's surprise, she was passed up for two paralegal spots she applied for in other departments of the firm. She couldn't figure out why, since Nathan was always praising her job performance, and saying "I don't know what I would do without you here to keep things going."

Finally an acquaintance told Gloria that she had better list some other references before Nathan if she wanted to get better recommendations. She had heard that Nathan was giving Gloria only lukewarm reviews with the senior attorneys who were hiring. Gloria did put some former bosses ahead of Nathan on her reference page, and was hired for the next opening for which she applied. In retrospect, she figured out that although Nathan could not or would not give her a *bad* reference because her work was known to be excellent, he was reluctant to give her a really enthusiastic review for one simple reason: He did not want to lose her.

If you are seeking promotion within your company or organization, or pursuing a better job elsewhere, be judicious about whom you tell and whom you give as references. It doesn't happen often, but sometimes people will undermine your advancement because they want to keep you for themselves. Sometimes selfish interests win out over integrity, and you have to be alert.

Set an Example of Collaboration

Some people withhold information or contacts even when they work for the same company as you and are supposedly on the same team. Be nuanced and political when you're seeking information and consider the ramifications that sharing has for the other people. Do they have valid reasons to keep the information to themselves? If so, respect those considerations. But if not—if you have a right to know—try these strategies:

- Go "Sherlock Holmes" or "Nancy Drew" on them. Be a professional and remember it's your job to get the information you need to do your job and move the company forward.
- Brace yourself to take some cruel words from someone who does not want you to have access, anything that might put you off or down so that you'll stay away from the information. Don't let their cutting words put you off the scent.
- Open up a line of communication by making yourself vulnerable, not to the degree that it's detrimental to you, but enough to encourage communication. For example, you might say, "Wow, you really know a lot about e-commerce. How did you learn so much?"
- You may have to swallow your pride to overcome communications blocks. It's amazing what can be accomplished when pride is put on the sidelines.

Susan was getting nowhere with Tom on a project that she knew could be extremely helpful for the company. She wanted simply to get onto the playing field with the information and contacts that she felt she needed. After a big meeting, she saw Tom talking to Joan, the CFO. Susan got up her nerve and walked over to Tom to ask a question, essentially to make small talk with the two of them so that the discussion might lead to the next steps that came out of the meeting. When Tom saw Susan, he turned his back and said, "Susan, would you mind? I've got something private that I'm discussing with Joan." Susan got a bit flustered and said, "Oh sure, I understand completely. Sorry," although she thought it was rude and knew that if she was in the inner circle Tom would have let her into the conversation with the CFO. Even if for a brief time he needed to discuss something private, he could have told Susan in a more tactful way.

Susan decided to let some time pass and to not take the incident personally. Tom had been promoted recently and she understood that she wasn't at his level yet and had to respect that fact. So she began to invite Tom to meetings that she had with very important clients and media types by whom she knew Tom would be impressed. Even though Tom never loosened up with Susan or brought her into any meetings, Susan kept inviting Tom to hers. She figured that if she could win his trust he might reciprocate.

Eventually Tom lost his position in a downsizing, but was still kept on as a consultant with the company. The tables had now turned. Tom *had* to start sharing his contacts and information with Susan because he was assigned to report to her! Susan didn't miss a beat. Once she was in a position of control she did not pull rank or become spiteful. She saw it as an opportunity to demonstrate the way she thought leaders should lead, and let everyone keep their dignity and pride.

Some people just don't know how to collaborate. Perhaps they have never been part of a team at work, participated in team sports, or even been part of a loving, cooperative family. The skills of collaboration and sharing don't come naturally to everyone and you might have to set an example.

Fear can also stymie collaboration. Some people are insecure about their positions or lack confidence in the value of their contribution to the organization. They think collaboration will undermine their position or lessen their value. Perhaps no one has ever done anything collaborative with them that had a positive outcome, and they expect that if they share, it will backfire.

In these cases, you have to model collaboration. Set an example. Share your own contacts and expertise. Help others overcome their fear of collaboration and the destructive tendency to be withholding. Also explain and demonstrate that there is a bottom-line business reason for collaborating. Show how the outcome will be positive for the company and how everyone, including them, will reap the benefits.

That said, there are some situations—when you're not in the same company but you know someone through an organization or other situation, for instance—where sharing is *not* appropriate. Some people must hold on to their contacts for professional reasons. Be sensitive and don't push if someone is reluctant. "You are who you know" can be taken very seriously, especially when it involves someone's client base. So that means working harder to develop and maintain your own contacts.

Women business owners, as a breed, are particularly generous about sharing contacts. Most respect each other and know there is enough business to go around, *if* we help each other grow.

The exponential growth of this collaborative attitude is part of a larger trend in the workplace to do well by also doing good. To me, the growth of corporate philanthropy and the recognition that supporting good causes is also smart business is a fulfilling affirmation of what I have always believed.

Change the World from Your Desk

I'll never forget when I was a college student and going through a period of soul-searching. I asked my father why someone would want to raise a child in this day and age, with so much selfishness and turmoil in the world. He looked me in the eye and told me from the heart: "The reason to have a child is so that she or he can change the world and make the world a better place." I have never forgotten how definite he was about his answer. And his words have given me direction ever since.

My mother also instilled in me early on the value that helping others is an unquestionable duty. In addition to raising five kids, she always found time to do a great deal of volunteer work in the community. My mother got me engaged in volunteer work when I was a teenager, and I found it tremendously satisfying. So I've always endeavored to find ways to give back, no matter how busy I am making a living.

Throughout my career, I have been motivated by my ideals. In fact, without ideals, there are really no career goals or life goals for me! However, in the same breath, let me admit that I'm no Mother Teresa. I like to travel, wear nice clothes, and even drive fast cars. And having known financial reversals in my family, I am highly motivated to ensure for myself that I have a secure financial future. So I've had to search for ways to pursue my heartfelt ideals, while also earning enough to enjoy a satisfying lifestyle.

I have always had an unrelenting—and many would say unrealistic—passion to change the world for the better through my work. So naturally, I thought of working for a nonprofit when I graduated from college. I landed at the American Cancer Society, where I earned $11,000 a year for a full-time job. Granted, it was a while ago, but it was still a very modest salary by any measure. I soon realized that the nonprofit world was going to be a little too nonprofit for my tastes—but I never gave up the idea of giving back. So no matter where I was working or how busy I found myself, I've always made time to stay involved in causes and organizations. And surprise—I found it was always a boon to business as well as imperative from a moral standpoint.

When I had my own public relations firm, I created (in collaboration with others) the Good Earth Festival for the Memphis Botanical Gardens, to educate people about composting, clean air, and so on. It was good for the environment and for the Gardens, bringing new visitors who then turned into dedicated contributors.

After I moved to Dallas to work in the hotel business again, I wanted to incorporate environmental green initiatives into the hotel marketing efforts. At the time, the industry was not ready for this approach, but later on they began to introduce green innovations into operations and marketing. From this experience I learned that you can't always get the response you want *when* you want it. And if you're working in a corporate setting, you can't shove your ideals down people's throats. Instead, you have to be sensitive to the atmosphere, plant your ideas, and sometimes wait until the soil is fertile for them to grow.

Remember: Frustrations, delays, and setbacks are inevitable when you're working toward something larger than your immediate personal needs. But if you believe in your cause and keep going, you'll see results. And meanwhile, it will have an energizing effect on your own life.

"Having a personal mission to pursue can be just as energizing as a creative urge," writes Rena Pederson, in her book *What's Next? Women Redefining Their Dreams in the Prime of Life.* "Having a mission orients, roots, and balances a person. It can give you a reason to get up in the morning and keep you going strong."

There are many great ways to change the world from your desk. Wherever you are in the hierarchy, whatever your limitations, you can still do something that makes a difference.

Participate in Established Corporate Philanthropy

Many corporations and organizations have a philanthropic outlet: a company foundation or a specific cause that the company supports through events and fundraising. Raise your hand and get involved! Ask how you can help, volunteer for a committee, and get other people in your department on board.

If you have ever volunteered, you know that helping is itself tremendously rewarding. But volunteering through your company is also a sound business move. Working together for a common cause is a great way to meet new colleagues, strengthen existing relationships, and expand your network. People will see what you can do on a volunteer level, and think of you for work-related opportunities.

Jump-Start a New Initiative

Muriel Siebert is founder and president of the Siebert Financial Corporation, which includes Muriel Siebert & Co., the discount brokerage firm. She was the first woman member of the New York Stock Exchange as well as the first woman superintendent of banking for the State of New York. And she is a role model in her commitment to corporate philanthropy.

In 1990 Muriel Siebert started the Siebert Entrepreneurial Philanthropic Program (SEPP). Under SEPP, half of the firm's net commission revenue on new issuer corporate underwritings is donated to a charity, usually chosen by the issuer or purchaser. Muriel Siebert has also developed an ambitious initiative to improve the financial literacy of the nation's young people, called the Personal Finance Program. It is currently being taught in New York City high schools and there is a drive to establish the program nationwide.

Now, I don't expect everyone to start anything of this scale. But that doesn't mean that you have to sit back and do nothing. You can start small. Ask ten people in your office to participate in a walkathon for heart disease. Get your company to buy some tables at a fundraising event. Hold a toy and clothing drive for needy children, and make it a yearly tradition.

Or, if you're in a position to do so, put forward a proposal for an affiliation with an existing organization, or for your corporation to set up its own foundation.

If you're introducing a charitable initiative, be judicious about which cause you select to support. Research what your customers care about. Is it helping the environment, health care issues, or making neighborhoods safer?

Also be sure that the cause is compatible with the business goals of the company. In the real world, there may be conflicts. For example, it might not be appropriate for your company to focus on environmental efforts, but they can support preschool education for disadvantaged children, or fight world hunger, or any number of other good causes. Be smart, be politic, and choose a cause that fits in with your customers' concerns and in no way conflicts with your corporate culture or product. This doesn't mean that you are compromising your ideals; it means that you're being strategic so that you can get something good done.

Take steps to ensure that coworkers will support your efforts. Do research within the company to find out what your employees want to support. Ask coworkers to lunch (perhaps one-on-one) to bounce ideas off them. Invite a boss for an informal cup of coffee to find out what causes she would like to see the company support.

Irene Malbin, vice president of public affairs for the Cosmetic, Toiletry, and Fragrance Association (CTFA), advises that you "Look for what your company is an expert at...and if there is a way that expertise can be used to help a charity or cause." For example, her association developed a program called "Work Your Image" with Women Work! (the national network for women's employment). The tagline is "Creating a professional appearance to get and keep a job," and the program draws on the professional expertise and resources of the beauty companies in CTFA.

Cause-Related Marketing

Cause-related marketing, or CRM, is an offshoot of traditional corporate philanthropy. According to The Foundation Center, "Cause-related marketing is defined as the public association of a for-profit company with a nonprofit organization, intended to promote the company's product or service and to raise money for the nonprofit."

Cause-related marketing can be very creative and versatile. It ranges from simple agreements to donate a percentage of the purchase price of a particular item to a charity for a specific project, to long-term and complex arrangements. "Corporations, too, have been drawn to CRM due to the competition of the expanding global marketplace and the need to develop brand loyalty," finds The Foundation Center. "A number of recent studies have documented that consumers carefully consider a company's reputation when making purchasing decisions and that a company's community involvement boosts employee morale and loyalty."

Often, women executives are particularly supportive of cause-related marketing efforts, recognizing their importance from both a business and personal standpoint. At Trinchero Family Estates (one of the 10 largest U.S. wine companies and owner of the Sutter Home brand), the company coowner, Vera Trinchero Torres, and the senior vice president of marketing, Terry Wheatley, both had been treated for breast cancer. Terry Wheatley was inspired to initiate the Sutter Home for Hope Campaign to support breast cancer research, treatment, and education. She linked the campaign to Sutter's white Zinfandel wine, which is actually pink like the breast cancer awareness ribbon. And in the fall months of 2004, Sutter donated $1 for every white Zinfandel cap that consumers mailed in to breast cancer research.

A cause-related marketing effort that is near and dear to my own heart is Wyndham's support of the Susan G. Komen Breast Cancer Foundation through the annual Dream For The Cure® program. In 2004, for example, Wyndham donated $1 to the organization for every reservation made from September 15 through October 31, and $10 on behalf of the first 1,000 guests who joined Wyndham ByRequest during October (which is Breast Cancer Awareness Month). We also placed specially designed pillow cards in our guestrooms with information on breast self-exams and early detection. Wyndham has raised over a million dollars for the Komen Foundation over the years.

"Consumers feel a connection with companies that support causes important to them," says Cindy Schneible, senior VP of the Komen Foundation. "To be successful in cause partnerships, companies must feel—and demonstrate—a genuine passion for or connection to the cause. Corporate social responsibility activated through cause partnerships benefits the company because it reinforces the brand reputation and message, and connects with customers. Also, employees feel a sense of pride when their employer takes up the banner of an important cause. It's a win-win-win situation for the corporate partner, the nonprofit, and the customers."

Giving Is Good Business

If you have ever volunteered, you know that giving is its own reward. You feel more alive when you help others. You feel more purposeful when you give back. It brings you outside of your daily concerns and gives you a higher purpose. It is highly satisfying, even therapeutic.

However, if you're promoting a new philanthropy or cause-related marketing effort in your company, you may need more than "feel-good" reasons to persuade management. You may need to convince the people in charge that giving back is also good for business. Fortunately, there is a wealth of data to back this up, especially when it comes to marketing to women.

A major Cone/Roper market research study found that:

- 84 percent of women have more positive images of companies that support causes
- 66 percent of women would switch brands or companies to those that support good causes
- 63 percent of women feel cause-related marketing should be standard business practice

The numbers are in and there's no shadow of a doubt that supporting causes is smart business. As the saying goes, "Who cares, wins."

The Next Step: Social Entrepreneurship

Just as the corporate world is expanding its philanthropic horizons, the nonprofit world is increasingly looking to corporate
strategies to run their organizations. Emily Eakin brought attention to this trend in her 2003 *New York Times* article entitled
"How to Save the World? Treat It Like a Business." According to
Eakin, "Social entrepreneurs are part of a new wave that mixes
capitalism with conscience." She cites inspiring examples of this
new breed such as Sara Horowitz, a lawyer and labor activist
who started Working Today, a group that provides low-cost
health insurance to freelancers. Another pioneer is Wendy Kopp,
who founded Teach for America, an organization that hires
young education graduates to teach in underprivileged urban
and rural areas.

According to David Bornstein, author of *How to Change the
World: Social Entrepreneurs and the Power of New Ideas*, the chief
characteristics of these visionaries are that they are "transfor-
mative forces." They are "people with new ideas to address
major problems, who are so relentless in the pursuit of their
visions that they will not give up until they have spread their
ideas everywhere."

The formalization of the concept of social entrepreneurship (it
is now taught in the top business schools) may be relatively new.
But men and women with vision to change the world have always
been around.

A famous example is Juliette Golden Low, founder of the
Girl Scouts in the United States. In 1912 she held the first
meeting with 18 girls. Now there are 3.3 million members!
Another pioneer is Mary McLeod Bethune, the fifteenth child
of former slaves, who worked her way up from the cotton fields
to attend college. In 1904, starting with $1.50 in cash, five pupils
and a rental cottage, she founded a school for young African-
American women that eventually grew into the Bethune-
Cookman College.

Make a Difference and Make a Profit

Another way to make a difference is by creating a for-profit service or product that improves the world—a lot or even a little. Adrienne Guillermo started a company that sells kits to car rental and hotel companies that adapt the vehicles or appliances for easier use by people with disabilities. Adrienne was raised by two deaf grandparents, and grew up determined to make a difference while expressing her entrepreneurial drive. She has won numerous awards lauding her work—and reaped financial rewards as well.

So even if you don't see yourself in the role of a world-shaking crusader, use your imagination. You can find a way to apply your energy and expertise to make at least one little corner of the world a better place.

Change the World from Your Desk— Whether It's a Cubicle or Corner Office

Check off which of these ways you can help:

- Volunteer to help with a philanthropy or foundation within your corporation.
- Propose or create a new philanthropic initiative in your organization.
- Support cause-related marketing efforts in your company.
- Educate bosses and coworkers about the benefits of giving back.
- Organize one small event to support a charity—it's a start!
- Introduce a new product or service that helps someone in some way.
- Support the work of social entrepreneurs.
- Join an organization that you believe in and contribute to the best of your ability.

Making Our Voices Heard

Locked away in the tower, Rapunzel sings to ease the pain of loneliness. When the prince happens to pass by and hears her voice, he falls in love with her sight unseen. "He rode home, but the song had touched his heart so deeply that he went into the forest every day to listen to it." In the world of fairy tales, where beauty is often emphasized, this is an unusual twist. Rapunzel's voice again brings them together at the end of the story, after they are both exiled to the wilderness and the prince is blind. "He heard a voice which seemed very familiar to him and he went towards it." They embrace, and "Two of her tears fell upon his eyes, and they immediately grew quite clear and he could see as well as ever."

The power of the female voices to attract, convince, and even heal is immense, in the real world as well as in fairy tales.

One way to make our voices resonate more in the business world is to raise them *together.* Terry Neese is president of Women Impacting Public Policy (WIPP), the nation's largest bipartisan public policy organization that advocates for women in business, with over half a million members. WIPP and its coalition partners work as a single voice to strengthen working women's sphere of influence in the legislative process, create economic opportunities, and build bridges and alliances. "Politics plays a role in our lives every day, at the office—at school, in the boardroom—and women must learn to band together," says Terry Neese. "It's that old 'power in numbers.' To be a player, one must learn how to strategize, understand how the business and political systems work, and work smart!"

Carolyn B. Elman, CEO of the American Business Women's Association, also emphasizes the importance of women banding together to make their voices heard. "If we want to be heard, we need to join together to craft messages which will get the attention of other women, corporations, and/or politicians. There is no doubt there is power in numbers, especially now that the business world, as well as politicians, recognizes the economic power of women."

Carolyn also notes the importance of communicating well within your own company. "On an individual basis, I think performance counts most. When you set goals which help advance the company's goals and consistently meet or exceed them in a visible way, you should expect to be heard in a company that values its team members."

Let Down Your Hair
and Make Your Voice Heard

- Strengthen your communication skills. Ask your mentor or a trusted colleague to help you evaluate your voice and improve it.
- Be a good listener. When you listen to others, they tend to reciprocate.
- Watch carefully how people who are good at getting their points across deliver their message and model their delivery.
- Take a course in public speaking if you need to improve your skills.
- Use humor to break down barriers. Take yourself seriously but keep a sense of humor and perspective.
- Join organizations that advocate what you believe in.
- Vote, write e-mails to government representatives, and make sure your opinion is counted.
- Use your buying power to patronize companies that support causes you believe in.

Through our voices and our compassion, we have the power to transform not only our own careers, but the workplace and the world at large. This is not a fairy tale, but a plausible reality that many women are striving toward every day. And it is gradually coming true as women collaborate, share our knowledge and resources, and make our voices heard.

$$\cdots\cdots\cdots\cdots\cdots\cdots\cdots\cdots\cdots\cdots\cdots\cdots\cdots\cdots\cdots$$

Rapunzel's Skyscraper

Once upon a time there was a girl who was fascinated with tall buildings. She grew up to be smart and strong, with fair hair that swept past her waist, and so her family called her Rapunzel.

After she graduated from college with a degree in structural engineering, she considered cutting her hair, but decided she enjoyed the distinctive signature look. So she coiled her long tresses into a braided bun and found a job at a huge engineering and architectural concern called Prince Unlimited (the owner was named Seymour Prince).

She hoped to work on their nationally famous skyscraper projects, but her supervisor, Mr. Gothel, told her that no one started at the top. Instead, she worked on structural analysis and design for people who wanted to build modern Victorians and other grand domiciles. Rapunzel became an expert in towers and turrets, cantilevered stories and sweeping staircases. But it was not the type of work she had envisioned for herself, so after a year of paying her dues she decided to speak to her boss.

"Mr. Gothel, how can I facilitate a move into the high-rise and skyscraper area of the firm?" she said. "Working on fancy houses is not why I became a structural engineer."

"Oh Rapunzel, why don't you let your hair down and relax," said Mr. Gothel. "Residential is a lot less stress than high-rise, where so many millions of dollars are at stake."

"Nonetheless, I would appreciate if you would make a recommendation to Mr. Prince..."

"That will never happen," said Mr. Gothel. "You're doing fine right here."

And so Rapunzel realized that she would have to go to Mr. Prince directly to pursue a new position. She set about preparing documentation of her training and experience, working surreptitiously. But one day her boss found a draft of an e-mail to Mr. Prince in her files.

Mr. Gothel was apoplectic. "You're plotting and planning to go over my head to Mr. Prince, even though I said you should stay right here in this department? Well, missy, the only place you're going is out of here altogether!" He fired her on the spot, saying he would tell everyone that she had been trying to steal clients and do projects as a moonlighter. Her name would be infamy in this firm and she'd be lucky to find a job anywhere in the industry.

Rapunzel found that it was, indeed, hard to find work in any of the top firms without a reference. She cut her hair to a chin-length bob, hoping it would give her a more professional demeanor, but it didn't make a whit of difference. And so she lived frugally on her small savings, wandering through job postings for a long time.

Finally she was hired by a nonprofit organization called HELM (Homes Evolving for Low-income Mothers) that built housing for disadvantaged single mothers. The salary was very low compared to her previous job, but Rapunzel found the work satisfying. She became deeply committed to the organization's vision of permanent housing being a starting point for women to rebuild their lives. In fact, Rapunzel became such an advocate that she was always asked to attend the meetings with potential funders. Her engineering expertise coupled with the passionate way she spoke about the organization's cause was very persuasive.

And one day who should she see at a meeting but Mr. Prince, whose firm was considering making a major donation to the organization. "You sound familiar..." he said.

"I used to work for your company," Rapunzel replied. And she told him the whole sad story of how she had been fired and framed by Mr. Gothel, who wanted to keep her for himself.

That's outrageous. I can tell from the way you made this presentation here today that you're a person of great integrity," said Mr. Prince. "I want you to come back to work for my company. And you can start working on skyscraper projects. Just because you're a woman, it doesn't mean you should be buried in residential."

Rapunzel considered the offer—a chance to work on her lofty dream structures, a salary more than double what she was making at the nonprofit organization—but she believed in the cause now and couldn't abandon it.

"I appreciate your offer and would love to accept it," she said. "But I can't just abandon HELM. Here's what I propose. I'll work on the skyscraper projects as my main focus. But I'll also facilitate an ongoing donor relationship between Prince Unlimited and HELM. What better way to show that you're a caring corporate citizen than to build low-cost permanent housing in the very cities where you build upscale high-rises!"

"I hear you," said Mr. Prince. "And I agree. It's an ideal philanthropic match." And so it was.

•••

Fairy Dust from *Rapunzel*

- Collaboration and networking are key to long-range career success.
- Set an example of collaboration and show people how it benefits everyone.
- There are many ways to change the world from your desk. Be creative and find the causes you are passionate about.
- When suggesting a new charity to your company, make sure it reflects the concerns of the customers and the other employees.

- Relate the cause to your corporation's areas of expertise and resources for the best results.
- By joining together in organizations, women in business can make their voices and concerns heard. Also, join organizations that include women *and* men.
- When we share knowledge and resources, women gain power to transform not only our careers, but the work world at large.

CHAPTER 10

....

Beauty and the Beast

Stand by Your Decisions, Take Risks, and Recognize Opportunity Like a CEO

THE HEROINE OF *BEAUTY AND THE BEAST* IS LEAGUES ABOVE MANY other fairy tale characters in maturity, and second only to Cinderella in sheer popularity. Beauty, or Belle, as she is called, is modern in her sensibilities: intelligent, an independent thinker, and a born leader. You can easily imagine her striding the halls of corporate America, speaking her mind, and rising to become a CEO after going through many tribulations.

It is not surprising to learn that *Beauty and the Beast* is the only famous European fairy tale that was first published by a *female* author (although many of the other tales came from the oral traditions of woman storytellers). Perhaps this accounts for the heroine's emancipated qualities. The first published version was a novella by Madame Gabrielle de Villeneuve, published in 1740. It was a complicated tale intended for the author's sophisticated salon friends, not for children, and included long digressions about fairy tale feuds and symbolic dreams. In 1756 Madame Le Prince de Beaumont, trimmed the tale into a short story. Andrew Lang's version of *Beauty and the Beast* in his 1889 *Blue Fairy Book* attributes the story to de Villeneuve, but also contains interesting elements of de Beaumont.

Beauty and the Beast has inspired a long succession of poems, novellas, short stories, and novels, as well as some of the best dramatic renditions in "fairy-taledom." The 1946 film by Jean Cocteau, *La Belle et la Bete,* is a masterpiece of cinematic surrealism, with primitive yet haunting visual effects such as candelabras made of living arms. Another adult version was the late 1980s CBS television show *Beauty and the Beast,* a cult favorite about the haunted love affair between a wealthy New York City woman attorney and a man/beast who dwells below the city streets.

But the image of *Beauty and the Beast* that has supplanted all others in the public imagination comes from the 1991 Disney hit, which won the Golden Globe for Best Picture and was nominated for a Best Picture Academy Award. The politically correct script plays up the qualities that make Belle so appealing to liberated women. She is depicted as a bookworm who dreams of escaping the provincialism of her little French village and refuses to marry a handsome but male chauvinist suitor. The Beast wins Belle's heart by honoring her intelligence and giving her access to his magical library. Then, in an act of bravery reminiscent of a civil rights activist, she defends the Beast against a gang of bigoted torch-bearing villagers who hate him because he's different.

The Disney film was adapted into a Broadway blockbuster, which has been seen by over 24 million people worldwide. The play has been performed in seven different languages and 15 countries. Belle is also one of the quartet of Disney Princesses who are seen on an infinite variety of merchandise, providing a guilt-free alternative to moms who worry that Snow White and Sleeping Beauty are too reliant on a prince's kiss. Belle is a solid role model for little and big girls: dedicated to learning, strong in her decision-making, and willing to take responsibility for her choices. Here is the outline of her story:

> *A merchant who has fallen on hard times embarks on an expedition to save his cargo. He asks his daughters what they would like him to bring back. The older girls ask for jewels and*

gowns, but the youngest (called Beauty or Belle), not wanting to burden her father, asks only for a rose. After a long and fruitless journey, the father gets lost and wanders into a strange, empty castle where he picks a rose for Belle. Suddenly, a terrifying Beast—the owner of the castle—appears.
He says that the merchant will die for his transgression, unless he brings him one of his daughters. "And she must come willingly," says the Beast. "See if any one of them is courageous enough and loves you well enough to come and save your life."

Back home, Belle declares she will take responsibility for her father's dilemma and save him. So she goes willingly to the Beast's castle. There, she is treated well by the Beast and finds many diversions: sumptuous gardens, tropical birds, a fabulous library, a music room, and a magical theater. But when the Beast asks her to marry him, she refuses.

Belle misses her family and asks to go visit them. The Beast tells her that she must return in two months, or he will die. Although Belle promises him that she will, after two months at home she delays her return. But when she dreams that the Beast is dying, she quickly uses the magical ring he gave her to be transported back. She revives the Beast, realizes that she loves him, and promises to marry him. Instantly fireworks light up the sky, the spell of enchantment is broken, and the Beast is transformed into a handsome prince.

Belle is a Beauty with brains. A rarity in fairy tales, the original story reveals her intellectual hunger when she finds a library in the Beast's castle where "…she saw everything she had ever wanted to read, as well as everything she had read, and it seemed to her that a whole lifetime would not be enough to even read the names of the books, for there were so many."

In the Disney movie and show, the other village girls think Belle is an oddball because she loves to read and dreams of going beyond the boundaries of her provincial life.

When Belle faces fearful difficulties she shows true leadership qualities: the ability to make difficult or unpopular decisions, and willingness to take responsibility for her decisions. By falling in love with the Beast before she knows that he's a prince, she also displays the vision to see potential and opportunity before others do.

Be a Leader at Any Level

Unlike Snow White or Sleeping Beauty, Belle is not born a princess—nor does she have a fairy godmother or a dozen dwarves to help her over the rough spots. Her father is a middle-class merchant who has fallen on hard times and her sisters are selfish harridans. Belle has no one to rely on except herself. But her innate leadership qualities bring her to a high position in a palace—with a prince who respects her autonomy, no less!

This fairy tale tells us that the finest characteristics of leadership are within the realm of anyone who has intelligence, integrity, courage, and persistence. Whether you're in an entry-level or mid-level job, or looking to make a major change, you can elevate your career by demonstrating leadership skills within your own parameters.

"There are leaders at every level," says Gail Evans. "If you have a passion and you believe you're a powerful person, you will be a leader. Not everyone can be at the top, so lead at your level. See what's needed at your level and act on it with your supervisor's blessing."

Marsha Firestone, president of the Women's Presidents' Organization, says that women in entry- and mid-level positions need to: "Think like you're the boss. Put yourself in your employer's shoes, regarding financial, human resources, and communications issues especially. Make a list of the things that your boss is responsible for. This will give you more of a global perspective on how your little piece fits into the bigger picture. After making the list, focus on developing yourself professionally. Are you a team player? Do you add value and offer creative solutions? Those who are successful and become CEOs do these things."

Make Difficult Decisions and Take the Heat

Belle never hesitates to stand by her decisions, even when they have unforeseen consequences. When her father relates how he roused the Beast's anger by picking a rose, Belle quickly rises to the occasion: "I have, indeed, caused this misfortune, but I assure you I did it innocently…" she says. "But as I did the mischief it is only just that I should suffer for it. I will therefore go back with my father to keep his promise." Belle might easily have tried to wrangle out of going to live in the Beast's palace in exchange for her father's freedom. But she goes of her own free will, determined to take responsibility for her decision without faltering. This demonstrates leadership at its best.

Leaders at any level must be able to make unpopular decisions, accept criticism without lapsing into defensiveness, and take the heat for failure and setbacks, even when they have the best intentions.

Over the course of my career, I've had to make many tough decisions: moving away from my family in my early twenties and relocating to Washington to work on Capitol Hill; starting my own business and then merging it with a larger one; pulling up roots yet again and moving to Dallas to be with my new husband and go to work for a hotel corporation. Then there have been the smaller, daily difficult decisions: who to hire, who to fire, when to give a project the green light, when to change direction because something is not working.

In all these decisions I've made—good, bad, and in-between—there is one common denominator: I never blame anyone else for the outcome. And I always make sure that the decision is my own, not someone else's idea of what I should decide. The flip side of taking responsibility is that I tend to be very tough on myself when one of my difficult decisions doesn't work out because I feel entirely responsible. I don't look for someone to blame because I know I made the choice. That's when support from my family and friends is so important.

When you make decisions, you must be prepared for success, failure, or something in between. If you try to cover every angle and wait until your success is guaranteed, you'll be paralyzed with inaction. Instead, try to look at every decision as an investment. Decisions are investments you're making in your career, your company, your job. You do your research, weigh the odds, and choose how to invest. If it doesn't work out, it's painful, but you have to take the loss in stride and figure out how to recoup.

Here's some advice from women in leadership positions on making and standing by tough decisions.

Be able to logically back up your decision. Patty Francy, treasurer and controller of Columbia University, oversees $2.4 billion in financial operations and $7 billion in assets. With this much at stake, she has to base her decisions on logic as well as judgment and experience. "My favorite course in college was logic, and what I learned in that class has served me well in decision-making," she says. "Preceding putting tough decisions in effect, one has to prepare and get comfortable with one's own logic, weigh alternative thinking, and then confidently go forward."

Once you make your decision, move ahead with assurance. "Self-doubt and fear of failure will prevent others from following," says Patty Francy. "Bravery feels good. Sometimes you are wrong, but you live through it."

Make Decisions Like a Leader
....

1. Do your homework. Research the issues and know the facts and figures.
2. Understand your own logic behind the decision.
3. Stand back and be objective, especially if your emotions are involved.
4. Anticipate criticism and be prepared to answer it.
5. Don't beat yourself up if the decision turns out to be wrong. Very few workplace decisions are a matter of life and death!

It is your role as a leader to rally the troops: your coworkers, bosses, board members, and customers. It's okay to admit you don't have all the answers. However, you need to project certainty that you will find the answers and meet the challenges.

Have a thick skin but a soft heart. Cheryl Pingel, CEO and cofounder of the multimillion-dollar company Range Online Media, points out that women are naturally people pleasers but must learn not to measure their worth by their "approval rating." She had this advice about learning to take a stand or go out on a limb: "We have to grow a thicker skin but still have soft hearts."

You don't have to abandon your innate kindness or leave your humanity at the door when you enter the world of leadership. Good leaders tap into their sense of compassion when they make decisions. There is nothing wrong with considering the effect on your employees, on the community, on your customers. Balancing the bottom line and the human impact is the core of compassionate leadership.

You can let people know that you have a heart without weakening your authority. In fact, consideration for employees will strengthen their loyalty and motivate them to work harder. Ruling by fear alone doesn't sustain motivation. Showing respect and consideration will build you into the kind of leader who lasts.

Be prepared for criticism. "With your visibility comes more criticism. If you don't want to be criticized then you don't want to be a leader," points out Candace O'Keefe, consultant to Leadership America. "There's a saying that if you have never been criticized, you have never done anything. I have learned, through experience, not to answer criticism with criticism. Literally take the high road. Stop and listen to the criticism versus reacting to it—because sometimes the criticism is valid."

Criticism is an opportunity to learn—*if* you can separate the emotional aspect from the professional and listen to criticism objectively. This is a tall order. Sometimes you just want to cry (and go ahead, but do it behind closed doors or wait until you get home). Once you've recovered your equanimity, however, consider how you can use the criticism constructively.

I've had people challenge me on points when I'm giving a speech...and sometimes rather rudely. At first I was shocked at what seemed to be bad manners, but then I started to look at these critical challenges as an exercise. It is a great discipline to learn to think on your feet and maintain your composure in the face of public criticism. Just like doing an extra-hard workout in the gym will build and tone your muscles, facing tough criticism will strengthen your resilience and leadership skills.

Remember that it's usually safer to hear criticism than to get no feedback at all. If you don't hear anything, you better believe that someone is probably talking behind your back. It is preferable to get the criticism out front where you can deal with it.

If you want to be seen as a leader, you have to prove that you're brave in combat. In a business setting, that means *inviting* criticism by asking for feedback. Send out an evaluation to an audience or a survey to customers. Write an e-mail to your supervisors or colleagues asking for their point of view on your decisions or actions. (But do this sparingly since you don't need your boss or colleagues to think you can't live with your own decisions.) You might hear some criticism that people would have kept to themselves if you hadn't asked. But it's worth the pain because it puts you in control of useful information. When you ask for the feedback, you take charge of it.

Move ahead with or without consensus. Leaders need to be able to make decisions with or without consensus. This is often a huge stumbling block for women, who gravitate toward group approval from early on. Listen to little girls playing, and you'll hear discussions about what to play first, who gets which doll, who has what role in a make-believe game. But young boys usually just pick up the toys they want and start playing, expecting that their buddies will either follow along or do their own thing. The boys are focused on action, not agreement.

In the business world, there are situations where consensus is required or advantageous, and other times when you'll never move forward if you wait for everyone to agree. You must be able to differentiate between these situations, and take the plunge if you need to move independently. This doesn't mean that you're not a team player, or that you're a queen bee. It means that you know you trust your own judgment, you've done your homework, and you're willing to take appropriate risks.

See and act as a visionary. Leaders must be visionary: They are able to see the big picture and move the company forward. Sometimes this means developing the vision yourself, other times it means sharing the vision of the CEO.

Judy Hendrick, Anne Raymond, and Elizabeth Williams are just a few of the remarkable women who have reported directly to a CEO at Wyndham. Judy Hendrick, who has spent over a dozen years at Wyndham as treasurer and chief investment officer, was hired by then CEO Jim Carreker and later reported to Fred Kleisner, who became CEO. "What I have seen is how a CEO handpicks people who will not only get the job done, but move the company forward. And each one of the direct reports to the CEO has to be mentally ready daily to make decisions and act accordingly as a direct extension of the CEO's vision," says Judy Hendrick.

Recognize Potential and Opportunity Before Others Do

Belle decides that she loves the Beast before she knows that he is really a prince. She sees past his feral appearance to recognize that he is good husband material, and is rewarded when the spell is broken.

One of the leadership qualities you can manifest on any level is the talent to recognize potential and opportunity before the rest of the crowd does. You can find the beauty in the beast by spotting potential in a person, a service, a product, or an idea. That's what successful CEOs do, and you can, too.

Here's how to see beneath the surface and bring out the best in people who work for you and with you:

- First, give people time to adjust to your style and to realize that you're not a threat.
- Find out what their professional aspirations are and consider those when assigning responsibilities.
- Look closely at people's talents and weak areas and give them work that builds on their strengths.
- Ask for their feedback. Let them know you have an open door and an open mind.
- Let people know that you recognize their value to the organization. Thank you's and praise will go a long way until it's time for raises and promotion.
- Offer ample opportunities for career development: additional training, workshops, and mentoring.
- Determine who wants to take on more responsibility and what they need to gain the confidence to do so.
- Give people who want to take on challenges a chance to learn, try, fail, and try again.

When it comes to seeing the potential in new ideas, inspiration springs from many places: your personal experience, clients, colleagues, friends, acquaintances, and sometimes sheer intuition. If you open up your awareness to these sources, you'll tap into a wealth of valuable ideas for new products, services, and businesses.

Pay Attention to Personal Experiences

Many successful businesswomen have found their niche by paying attention to what they themselves wanted and couldn't readily find. Donna Karan identified the need for modern, attractive clothing that would flatter a woman with a normal, not-so-skinny figure. Instead of creating fashions with models in mind, she designed with her own tastes as a template. She went on to build this idea into a multimillion-dollar fashion empire.

Sometimes inspiration comes from mundane experiences. Tamara Monosoff, a former business consultant who quit work to stay home with her baby, found herself constantly having to re-roll the toilet paper that her little girl unraveled onto the floor. So she invented a special latch that would secure the roll, and marketed it to parents of young children and pet owners. The idea took off and soon she added other items to her lucrative business. Denise Marshall designed an instant cooling bowl because she was tired of blowing on her kids' food to lower the temperature. She sold 20,000 of the bowls and then teamed up with an inventor of a nonspilling snack cup.

Ask for Feedback from Your Customers

At Wyndham, I've gotten some of my best ideas from taking the time to collect and examine information from the women who stay in our hotels. For instance, we found out that women often hesitated to order room service because they didn't like the idea of someone coming to the door at an unspecified time. A simple solution was to institute a policy where the room service waiter rings up approximately five minutes before he is ready to deliver the meal. That way the guest knows who it is when someone knocks on the door.

Companies routinely conduct market research and hire consultants to tell them what the customers want. But with all due respect to consulants, it's amazing what you can also learn from asking customers, talking to them, and putting yourself in their shoes.

Take Time to Listen to Coworkers

Be ready to listen to people at all levels in your organizations and you can glean some terrific information.

When I was handling publicity for the historic Peabody Hotel in Memphis, we sent out a survey to our food and beverage staff, encouraging employees to submit ideas. Well, I took the time to actually read the surveys, and I found a gem. A waiter suggested that we put on an IRS party on April 15—an Immediate Relief from Stress party. The idea was to get the post office and a large accounting firm to set up stations in the lobby of our grand hotel so that people could get last-minute advice and then turn in their tax forms. The Peabody would pay the cost of the stamps and offer drink specials. When we put on the party, the lobby was packed and the bar revenue increased about 1,000 percent. Most importantly, people gained awareness of the renovation of the historic Peabody Hotel, which in turn contributed to the renaissance of downtown Memphis. And all this stemmed from a waiter's suggestion that could easily have been overlooked. I learned that good ideas are all around us if we pay attention, listen to people regardless of their position in the hierarchy, and keep an open mind.

An extension of this attitude is to be ready to expand on other people's ideas. This is the soul of the collaboration and teamwork. When I was at the Peabody, my colleague suggested that we do a World Duck Tour with the Peabody Ducks to promote the meetings business. I took off with the idea and created the World Duck Tour jackets, then worked with Delta Airlines to have red carpets for the ducks to waddle down at each destination. The red carpet really got the media's attention, and in every city the television cameras were waiting for the ducks to arrive, resulting in terrific publicity for the Peabody and the airlines.

The Women On Their Way program at Wyndham was also the result of a group idea. It started with a dynamic team in the marketing department and a PR firm led by a terrific woman, Patrice Tanaka, and a great advertising agency, The Richards Group. The PR firm presented a good idea to hold a contest and to pinpoint a market segment of women business travelers. However, I championed this kernel of an idea and really made it into an industry-changing concept. Women's viewpoints and new products and services implemented from this one idea transformed how the travel industry values women today. I built on its success with a women's advisory board and national partnerships that really made it soar.

The moral is that you don't have to be a creative genius and come up with all the ideas yourself. You can also get stellar results by seeing the potential and opportunity in other people's ideas and expanding on them. Always be sure to give other people credit when it's due, of course. But also realize that you deserve credit for flying with the idea so that it realizes its full potential. People may accuse you of hogging the limelight or being a diva. But when you give your blood, sweat, and tears to a project and drive the results, you deserve the accolades.

Trust Your Intuition

In early versions of *Beauty and the Beast,* Belle dreams that she is visited by a lady who advises: "Try not to regret all you have left behind you, for you are destined to a better fate. Only do not let yourself be deceived by appearances." She tells Belle to let her heart guide her. And when Belle finally listens, she breaks the evil spell and finds fulfillment.

In business, there is a great emphasis on facts and figures, which is understandable, since real money is involved. But the role of intuition, or listening to one's heart, often gets lost in this welter of market research and measurable data. And that can be a detriment.

Women who are successful entrepreneurs as well as intrapreneurs within a corporation often have great intuitive powers. They *know* their ideas are right and this conviction gives them the power to get other people on board as financial backers and dedicated employees.

So don't turn a deaf ear to the voice of your intuition. Don't ignore what your heart is telling you. By all means, do your research and find out if there is solid evidence to back up your intuitive ideas. Study the numbers and don't jump in feet first because you have a gut instinct. But do *not* ignore the powerful resource of women's intuition. Usually the instinctive idea turns out to be the right one.

Lynn Robinson, author of *Compass of the Soul: 52 Ways Intuition Can Guide You to the Life of Your Dreams*, says, "One of the ways intuition communicates with you is through what you feel excited about. That's an important piece of input you should pay attention to, because it's providing you with information about a step that you could take. Begin to make time for it in your life."

Get Others on Board

As much as you might be tempted to control every aspect of implementation when you have a great idea, you need to bring others on board if you want it to take off. The more you allow others to feel that your new product, service, or project belongs to them, too, the more invested they will be in supporting you. And it's those alliances that will help you quell critics, get backing from the highest levels, and bring your idea to fruition.

Jane Robichaud, director of consumer and winemaking insights at Beringer Blass Wine Estates, is a leader in what has been traditionally a man's field. She made it to the top of this heady industry by coming up with innovative ideas, such as the Berginer Wine Tasting Wheels. "I've found it works better to bring others on board at the beginning as partners, not adversaries," she says. "Perhaps my best approach has been to lay out the ideas and get buy-in from an early stage, versus hogging all the information until the end and making people feel as if they were not part of the process. I've always liked to work as a team and I've really seen how being a good leader differs greatly from just being a manager."

"Make it part of your silent mission to bring people together," says Linda Clemons, CEO of Sisterpreneur and host of the radio show "Sister Talk." "A visionary can see how the story ends before the book is written, so if you have this gift, use it. This is especially important for women, and women of color in particular, to reach down and bring someone up with you as you climb the ladder." And if you do this, the story will have a better ending.

Slay the "Idea Killers"

It is inevitable that anyone who comes up with a valuable new idea will run into naysayers. As a leader, you have to be prepared to stay the course and maintain your conviction, even when you face opposition.

In his book *How to Become a CEO—The Rules for Rising to the Top of Any Organization,* Jeffrey Fox says, "Don't be discouraged by the idea killers...companies are full of them. They say things like, 'We can't afford it, we've tried that before...it won't work.' Don't give in. Don't let up. Idea people build businesses."

That doesn't mean you should summarily dismiss what the naysayers are saying. Instead, listen with an open mind. And listen carefully. Buried within their negativity, there are probably some valid points that you can use to improve your product, idea, or service. This approach will not only derail your critics, it will make your ideas stronger and more likely to succeed.

Take Risks and Enter the Castle

As Belle approaches the Beast's castle, colored lights begin to shine in all directions, fireworks blaze out, and the castle is illuminated from roof to ground. "In spite of her anxiety, she could not help admiring all the wonderful things she saw." As she explores inside, she finds rooms filled with precious jewels and fascinating diversions. The Beast's castle is like the work world: It looks intimidating, but women who are brave enough to enter can find many hidden treasures.

Starting Your Own Business or Organization

One of the greatest tests of courage is starting your own organization or company. Nancy Brinker, founder of the Susan G. Komen Breast Cancer Foundation, says, "The key is never to quit, *ever*, despite how fatiguing it can be, and how it sometimes seems like you can never reach the endpoint. If you don't project confidence and passion, how can you expect others to follow you? Also, you must see the big picture and not get bogged down in minutiae. It will weigh you down! It's important to remember that if you don't care who gets credit, it's amazing what you can get done!"

The biggest risk I ever took professionally was starting my own business. I quit a perfectly good job, had no guarantee of income, and started my own company without any financial backing. It was scary, but since I took that risk, all the others have seemed do-able. The experience raised my risk threshold and proved to be rewarding on many different levels.

Be forewarned, however, that there are a lot of fantasies about self-employment or entrepreneurship that may not pan out. You might make more money than at a salaried job, or even get rich, but your business also has a good chance of failing. You can have more flexible hours, but that doesn't mean you'll have more time for yourself, since business owners tend to put in more hours overall than salaried employees. There are many good reasons to strike out on your own, but money and freedom are not necessarily valid ones. You have to weigh the pros and cons carefully, and know your tolerance for risk.

Should You Enter the Castle?:
Assess the Risk of Going Out on Your Own
• •

Answer these questions to determine if you should consider self-employment or starting your own business:

(continued)

- Do you have a strong passion for your field or product?
- Do you feel comfortable making decisions on your own?
- Do you handle stress and uncertainty well?
- Do you know how to set and stay with your own priorities?
- Do you enjoy risks and challenges?
- Are you resilient and persistent?
- Have you thoroughly researched the market and your odds of success?
- Do you feel comfortable aggressively marketing yourself?
- Can you handle the stress of financial uncertainty?

"Yes" answers indicate an entrepreneurial profile. If you have more than one or two "no" answers, think carefully before you quit your job to start your own business.

Risk-Taking as a Stepping Stone

It is not only entrepreneurs who require a high tolerance for risk. People who aspire to leadership positions in any corporation or organization need to be risk-takers, too.

Risk-taking is often associated with devil-may-care male tycoons. But according to a special report on "Women to Watch" in the *Wall Street Journal,* women who are CEOs and top executives are "more likely than men to be risk-takers, as they've catapulted up the ranks after taking over troubled divisions that their male colleagues didn't want to run, and then turning those divisions around."

Leaders do not hesitate to take on incredibly difficult challenges and to risk failure. And they are not afraid to abandon secure jobs for high potential but riskier positions.

"I have always preferred risk-taking to comfort seeking, and have changed jobs and careers often," says Alair Townsend, publisher of *Crain's New York Business.* "I think it's important, especially in the earlier stages of careers, to consider moving around a bit while we can. Change broadens our experience and sharpens our focus on where our interests truly lie. And moving on often increases the odds of moving up."

Myra Hart took a risk and left a job at a food service retailer company as head of marketing to become one of the four founders of Staples. Myra then chose a second career in academia and now teaches in the MBA and executive education programs at Harvard. She advises: "Never join a company where you can't picture yourself being the CEO. For instance, once I was interviewing for a company and asked flat out, 'Could I ever be the CEO of this company?' The gentleman told me, 'Not if you don't have your engineering degree.' So I marked them off my list and moved on."

Assess the Risk of Taking a New Job
· ·

Answer these questions to determine if you should consider giving up a secure job to accept a position at a new company:

- Have you researched the new company's financial stability?
- Are they offering you a substantial raise?
- Are they giving you a contract that will cover severance if it doesn't work out?
- Will your present employer match or exceed the new company's offer?
- Do you have sufficient savings to cover three to six months of living expenses?
- Have you met and found that you like some of the new people with whom you'll be working?
- Do you believe in the new company's products/services?
- Do you feel that you'll fit into the new company's culture?

A majority of "yes" answers indicates that taking the new job is a good bet.

Another type of risk involves spearheading a new initiative at your present company. When it's your baby, your job is on the line, and it can be as risky as jumping to a new firm.

"When I was corporate VP of marketing for Sonesta Hotels worldwide, I said we could do a better job if we took advertising in-house and produced ads ourselves," says Irma Mann. "So I became president of a wholly owned subsidiary of Sonesta, an advertising agency named S/I/A. The risk was that I had virtually no experience in organizing and running an advertising agency. If I failed, I could have lost my VP-marketing job and cost the company an enormous amount of money. That didn't happen...we were very successful and were the first hotel company in the world to have our own in-house agency. What I learned was to dare to be audacious. Without risk, it's hard to grow."

Like so many other women in the workforce (and Belle), I entered an intimidating environment of my own free will. The corporate world seemed as scary as a dark forest and as unpredictable as a castle under a spell. And although I entered willingly, for a long time it still felt like a prison, and I secretly dreamed of a prince to carry me away from the burden of earning a living. But gradually a transformation took place. I discovered that I could find knowledge, power, and fulfillment in the business world. If you have the courage to enter and the fortitude to keep exploring, it can be a very rewarding adventure.

....

The Beauty Business and the Beast

Belle worked in the branding department of a large cosmetics firm. The company had generated a storm of criticism from conservative groups because their last ad campaign featured teenage girls in garish makeup and tawdry clothes. So Belle came up with an idea for a new line that would serve as an antidote to the negative publicity. "It's going to be called 'Rose,'" she proposed at a brainstorming session. "It's pure, nostalgic, and reminiscent of young ladies dreaming through languid summer afternoons in the countryside."

Belle's boss loved the idea and took it to the top, where it was given the go-ahead with high hopes. But developing the petal-shaped packaging went way over budget. And the "English Rose" starlet who was hired to be the face of the line demanded a small fortune. Then, after a costly launch, the products failed to catch fire and the line turned out to be a dismal flop.

"Management wants someone from branding to go to the board meeting and explain why we went with the 'Rose' concept," Belle's boss announced after the debacle. "I guess it's going to be my head on the chopping block."

"No, it was my idea, and I'll take the heat," said Belle. "I'll go before the board."

The night before the board meeting, Belle was sick with anxiety. She couldn't eat dinner or concentrate on helping her teenage daughter with her algebra homework.

"You are, like, so stressed out, Mom," said her daughter. "If your job is making you so crazy, why don't you just look for another one?"

"It's not so easy," said Belle. "I'm 45 and beauty is a young industry. Anyway, I enjoy my job and I want to keep it."

Once Belle was before the board, a rush of adrenaline lifted her spirit. She explained without apologies the rationale behind 'Rose,' and showed the market research that had supported their decision to launch the line. She made a case that although the line was not a big seller, it had served a purpose by redeeming the company's image as a good, moral corporate citizen. The tradeoff was that people turned off by the sleaziness of the previous ad campaign were comfortable with the firm's products once again, and the bottom line would benefit in the long run. In addition, they had a new concept that was sure to be a huge success and more than compensate for the Rose line's lackluster performance. And they would be announcing the new concept soon.

Belle left the board pacified and eager to cultivate the new idea. Then she went home and lay awake all night, trying to think of what this new concept could possibly be.

In the morning, Belle put on her concealer in a vain attempt to cover the dark circles under her eyes. Then she searched for her eye shadow. "Did you take my makeup again?" she asked her daughter. "I asked you not to do that. You have your own."

"Well, what difference does it make? It's all the same stuff, isn't it? Anyway, Mom, no offense, but I really don't think that sparkly type eye shadow works for you anymore. It accentuates the wrinkles."

Belle snorted, rustled through her daughter's makeup bag, and dabbed on the eye shadow. Then she peered closer to the mirror to take a look at herself (because she was starting to need glasses.) Well, smart-alecky as her daughter was, she was right—the shadow was all wrong.

And then it hit Belle like a burst of fireworks. She knew what the new makeup line should be: "Prime—makeup that works at any age, for professional women over 45."

At first, her boss resisted the idea. "But it's been tried a hundred times and it doesn't work. The over-45 market is a beast. Mature women don't want old-lady makeup. They want to look young. Or they lose interest in makeup and just keep using the same stuff they've used since they were 25."

But Belle knew in her heart that it was the right timing for this new line. Her generation of women had challenged the status quo every step of the way, and they were ripe to rebel against the pressure to look silly by looking too young. They were ready to liberate the allure of the older woman. Plus, there was the aspect of sheer vanity. Wearing the same makeup as young women was simply not the most flattering option. The company would run free clinics to educate mid-life women on how to redo their look. Americans would learn to cultivate the continental appreciation of "women of a certain age."

In love with her idea, Belle went on with credible reasoning until her boss saw the light.

At first it was a hard sell to the higher-ups, who were attached to the idea that older women only wanted to look younger. But with fervent conviction, focus groups, and intensive market research to back them up, Belle and her boss eventually convinced the higher-ups that Prime was worth a gamble. And it paid off big-time. The media lit on to the novel concept of being beautiful without looking young.

Sales soared as women flocked to claim their right to a new age of beauty.

Belle was named Head of the Prime Division and given a healthy raise. Now she could put away money toward her daughter's college, and her own eventual retirement.

But first she faced the daunting challenge of keeping the momentum of the brand going.

....

Fairy Dust from *Beauty and the Beast*

- You can be a leader at any level.
- Leaders must make difficult decisions and take responsibility for both failure and success.
- Look at decisions as investments. Do the research, weigh the odds, and if it doesn't work out figure out how to recoup any losses.
- With greater visibility comes more criticism. Don't judge your success by your approval rating.
- Don't emphasize your fears and doubts if you want others to follow.
- Have a thick skin but a soft heart. Compassion is a key element of good leadership.
- Find the beauty in the beast by spotting potential in a person or idea before others do.
- Be rational but also listen to your heart. Intuition is a powerful tool.
- Moving on to a new job or business increases the odds of moving up.
- If you stand by your decisions, recognize opportunities, and take risks, you can go all the way from Cinderella to CEO!

Organizations and Resources

Alliance of Technology and Women (ATW) works to empower women in technology. They provide education on trends, networking connections, and mentoring. *www.atwinternational.org*

American Business Women's Association brings together businesswomen of diverse occupations and provides opportunities for women to grow personally and professionally through leadership, education, networking support, and national recognition. *www.abwa.org*

American Women In Radio & Television (AWRT) advances the impact of women in the electronic media and allied fields by educating, advocating, and acting as a resource to its members and the industry. *www.awrt.org*

The Association of Women in Communications champions advancement of women across all communications disciplines, including print and broadcast journalism, television and radio production, film, advertising, public relations, marketing, graphic design, multimedia design, and photography. *www.womcom.org*

Blue Suit Mom provides articles, information, and resources for working mothers. *www.bluesuitmom.com*

Boardroom Bound is a public service to provide services to help companies find prequalified women and minority candidates for corporate board service. *www.boardroombound.biz*

Business and Professional Women/USA promotes equity for all women in the workplace through advocacy, education, and information. They also offer opportunities to support scholarships for disadvantaged women. *www.bpwusa.org*

Business Women's Network/Diversity Best Practices is a premier source of information, resources, contacts, and opportunities helping women and diverse individuals and companies expand their horizons. *www.bwni.com*

Catalyst conducts research on all aspects of women's career advancement and provides strategic and Web-based consulting services on a global basis. *www.bwni.com*

Center for Women's Business Research Center works to unleash the economic potential of women entrepreneurs by conducting research, sharing information, and increasing knowledge about this fast-growing sector. *www.womensbusinessresearch.org*

Count-Me-In provides access to business loans, consultation, and education. The first online microlender, Count Me In makes loans of $500 to $10,000 available to women across the United States. *www.count-me-in.org*

www.cinderellaceo.com Share information with other readers of *From Cinderella to CEO* and other web sites to help you in your quest to transform your work life.

85 Broads was originally founded as an independent global network for current and former Goldman Sachs women professionals. In 2000, their "comentoring" initiative, Broad2Broad, was launched for current women MBAs at many of the leading business schools in the United States and Europe. *www.85Broads.com*

eWomenNetwork is a community of women who want to provide unlimited opportunities to transact business with women. *www.ewomennetwork.com*

The Executive Women's Golf Association (EWGA) provides opportunities for women to learn, play, and enjoy the game of golf for business and for life. *www.ewga.com*

Leadership America recognizes, educates, and connects accomplished and diverse women to increase their individual and collective impact globally. *www.leadershipamerica.com*

Minority and Business Women Enterprise is creating the nation's largest, most comprehensive database of minority and women business enterprises to encourage and support their growth and success. This database provides local, regional, and national exposure to both public and private sector supplier diversity managers. *www.MWBE.com*

National Association of Female Executives (NAFE) is dedicated to the success of women in business through networking. *www.nafe.com*

National Association of Women Business Owners (NAWBO) represents the interests of all women entrepreneurs in all industries, and is affiliated with *Les Femmes Chefs d'Entreprises Mondiales* (World Association of Women Entrepreneurs) in 35 countries. *www.nawbo.org*

Susan G. Komen Breast Cancer Foundation works through a network of U.S. and international affiliates, and events like the Komen Race for the Cure®, to eradicate breast cancer as a life-threatening disease by funding research grants and supporting education, screening, and treatment projects in communities around the world. *www.komen.org*

Vote, Run, Lead is a national nonpartisan initiative of The White House Project devoted to advancing women's leadership by igniting and mobilizing the power of women's political leadership. *www.voterunlead.org*

The Women's Foodservice Forum engages the food service industry to develop leadership talent and ensure career advancement for executive women. All segments of the industry are reflected in the membership. *www.womensfoodserviceforum.com*

Women's Funding Network is a worldwide partnership network of women's funds, donors and allies. *www.wfnet.org*

Women Impacting Public Policy (WIPP) is a national bipartisan public policy organization representing more than 505,000 women in business and women business owners nationwide. *www.wipp.org*

Women's Leadership Exchange (WLE) helps to develop more women leaders in business and other areas of human endeavor by connecting women with top business experts, corporate leaders, and with each other. *www.womensleadershipexchange.com*

Women's Leadership Initiative/Meeting Professional International is the touchpoint for research, education, mentoring and networking for and about women in the meeting industry. *www.mpiweb.org* and *www.wli.mpiweb.org*

The Women's Museum: An Institute for the Future is devoted to providing a public forum for the celebration and communication of the immeasurable contributions women have made to society. As the only comprehensive women's museum in the United States, it focuses on American women. *www.thewomensmuseum.org*

Women's President's Organization is a nonprofit membership organization for a diverse group of women presidents who have guided their businesses to at least $2 million in gross annual sales (or $1 million for a service-based business). *www.womenpresidentsorg.com*

Women On Their Way provides travel tips, a newsletter, articles, and links to women's organizations especially geared toward women business travelers. *www.womenontheirway.com*

Women Work! is dedicated to empowering women from diverse backgrounds and helping them achieve economic self-sufficiency through job readiness, education, training, and employment. *www.womenwork.org*

Index